LANGUAGE AND LANGUAGE LEARNING

Five inaugural lectures

LANGUAGE AND LANGUAGE LEARNING

Edited by R. MACKIN   P. D. STREVENS

W. SIDNEY ALLEN   C. E. BAZELL

R. QUIRK   N. C. SCOTT   P. D. STREVENS

Five inaugural lectures

Edited with a Foreword by

PETER STREVENS

Professor of Applied Linguistics
in the University of Essex

London

OXFORD UNIVERSITY PRESS

1966

Oxford University Press, Ely House, London W.1

GLASGOW NEW YORK TORONTO MELBOURNE WELLINGTON
BOMBAY CALCUTTA MADRAS KARACHI LAHORE DACCA
KUALA LUMPUR HONG KONG CAPE TOWN SALISBURY
IBADAN NAIROBI LUSAKA ADDIS ABABA

Printed and bound in Great Britain
by the Camelot Press Ltd., London and Southampton

Contents

Editor's Foreword

This book contains a collection of five Inaugural Lectures delivered in British universities between 1957 and 1962 in the fields of Phonetics, Linguistics, and the study of the present-day English language. Not all British universities maintain the practice of requiring a Professor to give a public lecture soon after he is appointed to a Chair, but in the universities where the custom is observed the Inaugural Lecture becomes a notable occasion, at once personal and professional, academic and public. On these occasions the university displays to its own members and to its friends outside its walls the quality of its newly-appointed member; the public has a rare opportunity of hearing a set-piece lecture by a specialist; the new Professor has a chance to talk about his subject (or indeed about any subject he cares to select) to a large and captive audience. It is an occasion where the choice of theme lies with the Professor himself: he may extol the virtues of his predecessor; he may prepare the ground for a change of emphasis in his department; he may give a *compte-rendu* of the state of his discipline; he may lay the foundations of goodwill and good public understanding of his needs that will precede a campaign for more money, or staff, or equipment; or he may make his Inaugural Lecture a contribution in itself to the scholarship of his subject.

In the lectures reprinted here, traces of all these motives may be discerned, but that is not the reason for collecting them within one cover. Their merit as a collection is that they illustrate some of the important trends in the linguistic sciences which have developed in Britain during a short but crucial period.

The lectures are presented in chronological order. The first is by Professor W. S. Allen, whose appointment to the Chair of Comparative Philology at Cambridge was important for two reasons: in the first place it created a valuable link between the different yet cognate traditions of classical and philological studies on the one hand and the newer discipline of linguistics on the other; it also established modern linguistics for the first time in either of our ancient universities.

The second lecture is one of two having a connection with the retirement of the late Professor J. R. Firth from his post in the University of London School of Oriental and African Studies. Firth had been Professor of Phonetics and General Linguistics but this title was not continued after his retirement. Professor Bazell was appointed to a Chair of General Linguistics and somewhat later Professor Scott was appointed to a Chair of Phonetics: both their Inaugural Lectures are included here.

The third lecture in this volume is that of Professor Randolph Quirk. The importance of his Chair lies, in part, in the way in which he (like Professor Allen) has combined an established reputation in philology—Quirk is a distinguished scholar in Old and Middle English—with the application to his field of the theories and techniques of modern descriptive linguistics. The *Survey of Contemporary English Usage* which Professor Quirk is conducting at University College London, together with his close connexion at the same College with the Communication Research Centre (Director, Dr M. A. K. Halliday) are evidence of this happy combination. They illustrate, also, the keen interest currently taken in the study of the present-day English language by means of techniques perhaps more insightful and illuminating than conventional descriptive procedures now appear to be.

The fourth lecture is by Professor N. C. Scott and it emphasizes another strand common to all these papers. Professor Scott is a phonetician in the tradition of British phonetics which goes back at least to Henry Sweet but which was especially identified with Professor Daniel Jones. Linguistics in Britain presupposes a strong basis of general and descriptive phonetics; all the authors represented in this book received such a basis but Professor Scott is the only one among them to be a professional specialist in this particular area.

The last lecture is my own, delivered at Leeds and describing the background to the study of Contemporary English, then newly established there. Although I am no longer at Leeds the lecture may perhaps stand as a further testimony to the interpenetration in British universities of phonetics and linguistics, the study of the present-day English language, and indeed the whole wide range of disciplines that come under the general label of 'applied linguistics'.

PETER STREVENS

University of Essex
August 1964

On the Linguistic Study of Languages

An inaugural lecture delivered on 8 March 1957 by
W. SIDNEY ALLEN, *Professor of Comparative Philology in the University of Cambridge*

On the Linguistic Study of Languages

Author's Note
An inaugural, as I have commented in this lecture, is a personal occasion, and calls for something other than the reading of just another paper. Its contents and style, moreover, are relevant to a particular time and place and should therefore be viewed in the light of their context. In Cambridge in 1957 Linguistics was recognized only by the existence of an optional paper in the Modern and Medieval Languages Tripos, and by the election to the chair of Comparative Philology of one who had served his apprenticeship under the late Professor J. R. Firth at the School of Oriental and African Studies in London. It seemed at the time, therefore, that a rather vigorous form of statement would be needed if Linguistics were to be recognized as an autonomous discipline and not a mere appendage of traditional philology; and if this requirement resulted in some degree of over-simplification, and even over-statement, it may perhaps be excused by the circumstances.

In 1965 the situation is already different. Linguistics is now modestly established in Cambridge. There is an inter-faculty General Linguistics Committee, and an option in the subject is available in Anthropology and in all the language Triposes except English. There are lectureships in General Linguistics and in Phonetics, and a well-equipped phonetics Laboratory. With the co-operation of the Mathematical laboratory, a linguistic computing centre has recently been established. Plans for language laboratories are well advanced, and the necessity for their integration with linguistic research has been recognized by the proposal of a post in Applied Linguistics. There is a senior Linguistic Society and a flourishing junior Linguistics Club. It will therefore be appreciated that much of what is said in this lecture it would now be unnecessary to say, and most of it could be more subtly expressed.

A few particular points call for some comment in retrospect. On p. 20 I said that 'The linguist is concerned with the actual and not with the possible'. This remark was directed primarily at the 'linguistic' philosophers' sometimes cavalier treatment of natural language. But in 1957 appeared Chomsky's influential work

3

Syntactic Structures; and writing after 1957 one would certainly wish to enter a caveat to this statement, making it clear that one's argument is not with the theory of generative grammar, which is intimately concerned with the potential of language, seeking as it does to account for the speaker's ability to construct an infinity of sentences and to understand those he has never heard before.

The stimulus of Chomsky's work has also had the effect of nullifying my criticism of the cut-and-dried 'proceduralism' of transatlantic linguistics (p. 16), since it has resulted in a ferment of theoretical discussion which seems likely to continue for some time to come.

Finally there is one statement which seems to have acquired a certain notoriety, namely (p. 12): 'There are no facts in linguistics until the linguist has made them'. To a minority of hearers and readers this seemed an alarming statement, carrying suggestions of cooking the data to suit one's theories. But of course, as was generally recognized, this was not its intention; it was an abbreviated and, I hoped, effective way of saying that one's description will vary according to the conceptual framework that is brought to bear on the data (which are emphatically inviolate), and that this framework is the linguist's creation and not itself inherent in the data. In fact it simply expresses a relativistic view of linguistic theory, and becomes scandalous only if 'language' is substituted for 'linguistics'.

Linguistic science in the twentieth century may count amongst its characteristics a critical attitude towards previous linguistic activities, and a growing awareness of its own theoretical foundations. In the words of the Danish theoretician, Louis Hjelmslev, the linguistics of the past—even of the recent past—has concerned itself with 'the physical and physiological, psychological and logical, sociological and historical precipitations of language, not language itself'.[1] For the primary expression of this criticism we are indebted, as in so many points of theory, to the Geneva comparatist and general linguist, Ferdinand de Saussure: the final chapter of his *Cours de Linguistique Générale*, posthumously compiled from his

[1] *Prolegomena to a Theory of Language*, p. 2.

4

pupils' lecture-notes between 1906 and 1911, ends with these words: 'Linguistics has but one proper subject—the language-system viewed in its own light and for its own sake.'

But it was, as Hjelmslev remarks, 'a long way from plan to execution'; de Saussure neither himself achieved nor lived to see the liberation of linguistics from its traditionally ancillary status. And even today, as we throw off one improper allegiance we are confronted by other diversions of a no less insidious nature.

This state of continued crisis is by no means to be deplored: of a 'crisis' in linguistics we may cheerfully exclaim with Hugo Schuchardt, 'Das ist ein gutes Wort!'[1] But the situation suffices to justify the title of this lecture: the epithet 'linguistic' is necessary in order to differentiate the proper study of language material from the various other studies that threaten to obscure it, and from those related activities of a less *sui generis* character which are conveniently designated in English by the term 'philology'. Whilst the titles as such—'linguistics' and 'philology'—are unimportant, they serve to maintain a basic distinction which has been specifically emphasized by linguists as diverse in outlook as de Saussure[2] and Leonard Bloomfield.[3] But it is well known that the rubric under which linguistics is pursued in several universities of the English-speaking world is that of 'comparative philology'—thereby reflecting a tradition of the nineteenth century. The occupant of a chair thus labelled may in fact handle both the nineteenth- and the twentieth-century disciplines—the former primarily in teaching and the latter in research—but although some degree of cross-fertilization is both inevitable and desirable, the linguistic (or philological) Jekyll is not therefore to be confused with the philological (or linguistic) Hyde.

---

[1] *Brevier*[2], p. 451.   [2] *Cours*, p. 21.

[3] *Language*, p. 512; cf. G. M. Bolling, *Language*, v, pp. 27 ff. ('Linguistics and Philology').

One school would go so far as to reject even the title of 'linguistics' (in favour of 'glossematics'), on the ground that linguistic studies thus far have failed to perform their true functions.[1] Such an attitude, however, seems ill advised unless one enjoys the full certainty that one's own activities have avoided all the snares that beset one's predecessors, as well as those that are constantly coming into being. It is sufficient if we maintain the opposition of 'philology'/'linguistics' to differentiate the study of language as a means from that of language as an end in itself—regardless of whether its theoretical aims are or are not completely fulfilled in practice.

But it may reasonably be asked of the linguist that he should give a more positive, and not simply oppositive, meaning to the terms 'linguistic' and 'linguistics', by defining his attitude towards certain fundamental matters, such as the nature of his material, his undefined presuppositions, and the methods appropriate to his subject.

A difficulty here arises, in that the subject is still in a state of development; linguists are still only working towards agreement on points of basic theory, and there are many matters on which argument is still vigorous. It does in fact seem that unifying trends are gradually prevailing over the fissiparous, but still a linguist's *credo* must be a more or less personal composition, the recital of which is perhaps best suited to a personal occasion.

A recent publication contains a comprehensive statement of the sphere of linguistic studies: 'Linguistics is concerned with language in all its aspects—language in operation, language in drift, language in the nascent state, and language in dissolution.'[2] *Linguista sum, linguistici nihil a me alienum puto!*

[1] *Prolegomena*, p. 51.
[2] Jakobson and Halle, *Fundamentals of Language*, p. 55.

6

But even the adherents of so catholic a creed would probably agree that their primary concern was with 'language in operation'; the less catholic might maintain that 'language in the nascent state' (referring to the process of learning) and 'language in dissolution' (referring to the condition of aphasia) belong rather to the domains of psychology and neurology; and some at least would feel that 'language in drift' (referring to its historical development) is hardly to be grouped with its synchronic, operational aspect. It may, then, be objected that the adoption of so diffuse a definition of linguistics runs the risk of precluding any unified theory, such as would justify its status as a subject, rather than an ill-defined field of activities connected with language.

The reference in the present title to the study of languages rather than of language is not unmotivated. It is intended to emphasize the view that, for all the generality of one's theory, it is to specific languages that it is applied; and it is by its ability to handle the specific language-materials that its validity is to be judged. There is indeed no lack of statements about language in general; and there is a tradition that the linguist should crown his life's work with a definitive volume entitled, with noble simplicity, 'Language'. Whilst the importance of many such works is beyond doubt, their value is in inverse proportion to their fulfilling the promise of their title; their influence on the development of our subject depends upon their dealing in fact with languages and with the principles of linguistics, rather than with the vague generality of 'language'.

General statements about language tend, when they are not simply trivial, either to be *a priori* and experimentally unverifiable, or else founded upon an extrapolation from the writer's own more or less limited experience. On the grammatical side in particular, they tend to be expressed in terms of a traditional

7

framework that is presumed to have universal relevance: the linguistic categories established for Greek by Greek philosophers and grammarians were, as is well known, uncritically transferred to Latin; and the Middle Ages saw the elevation of these categories to the universal status which they have done nothing to deserve. In Hjelmslev's words, 'The specific forms of expression peculiar to Greek and Latin had fatal repercussions on European grammar: a single morphological type—a type unique in the world—determined the structure of the theory.'[1]

It is indeed questionable whether any scheme of universal categories can profitably be established. But if we reject this possibility, it does not mean that we have no general theory; the distinction has been summarized by J. R. Firth, who speaks of 'a *general linguistic theory* applicable to *particular linguistic descriptions*, not *a theory of universals* for *general linguistic description*'.[2] It is precisely the existence of a theory, or (if we consider our present internal disagreements) the existence of the several theories, that makes linguistics a rather different matter from, for example, the more inductive activity of philology. The broadest outlines of such a theory I shall indicate in considering the question of 'meaning'.

Linguistic categories result from the application of the general theory to the specific languages. And it may happen that we employ the same labels to refer to categories established for different languages. But this is basically a matter of terminological and typographical economy—and it is at our peril that we make any linguistic identification of the homonymous terms. To identify the categories called 'Verb' in analyses of Russian and of Chinese could not be other than misleading— as also, at the phonological level, would be an identification of the phonemes /t/ in English and /t/ in Urdu simply because

[1] *Ve Congrès Intern. des Linguistes* (Bruxelles, 1939), *Extrait des Rapports*, p. 79.
[2] *Studies in Linguistic Analysis* (special volume of the Philological Society, 1957), p. 21.

in our analysis we decide to write them both with the same letter. One practical consequence of such false identification may be mentioned; the phonetic confusion of the Urdu and English categories in question was in fact a traditional solecism of the British in India—and phonetic solecisms are no more pardonable in their perpetrators, or less discourteous to their hearers, than the more generally reprehended errors of grammar.

If the linguist is to remain true to his purpose of seeking those modes of statement which are most appropriate to the particular material he is handling, he must be prepared to discard even such general categories as, by their wide attestation, seem likely to reflect universals. But so strong are our traditions that the jettisoning of old prejudices, and the achievement of a conceptual *tabula rasa*, is often a more difficult task than the erection of new frameworks of description. Recent researches on a language of the NW Caucasus suggest that in phonological analysis even the traditional trio of Consonant, Vowel, and Syllable may not be universally applicable—if one tries to apply it, one is left with the uneasy feeling that the statement is less elegant than the material deserves. A proposed solution shows more affinity to the Arabic writing-system than to the Roman which has moulded so much of our phonological thinking.[1]

It is perhaps obvious that linguistics does *not* include what Henry Sweet, in an excellent work devoted to it, called the *Practical Study of Languages*. Facility in the *use* of languages is no necessary concern of our discipline. It is of course true that a familiarity with many languages—and the more diverse the better—may do much to reduce the ethnocentrism with which, as native speakers of a language, we are inevitably burdened; for no one who has not had some considerable

[1] Allen, *Transactions of the Philological Soc.* 1956, pp. 170 ff.

experience of this kind is likely to surmount the provincialism imposed upon him by the peculiarities of his own tongue, or by the traditional scheme of categories. And actual facility in the use of foreign language is of course essential in dealing with monoglot informants—who, from some points of view, represent a theoretical ideal; but this is an incidental administrative matter, without relevance to linguistic analysis as such.

The phonetic performance of crucial items, on the other hand, is a basic essential of linguistic study. We are handling a facet of social behaviour which is only partially accessible to inspection; we hear the sounds, we can record them, and we can analyse them instrumentally in various ways; but the performative side of the activity, the acts of phonation with their delicate and complex muscular movements, are largely invisible to normal observation, and only partially observable by instrumental means (which tend, in any case, to impose artificial conditions and inhibitions upon the speaker). The ability to translate sound heard into terms of sound made—a peculiar exercise of the kinaesthetic faculties—comes only by submission to the discipline of phonetics; and even for the trained phonetician the only check upon his analysis is to put that analysis into reverse—to convert it into utterance in his own mouth—and to observe whether it is accepted as valid by the critical native performer.

A more debatable question is that of the relevance of the historical process to linguistics. We have inherited from the nineteenth century a peculiar obsession with time and with origins. As Marc Bloch has observed in his *Apologie pour l'histoire*, 'The explanation of the nearer by the farther has sometimes dominated our studies to the point of hypnosis' (p. 5). The historical, genetic study of language owed much to the direct influence of Darwinian biology; much has already been written on the illegitimacy of the analogy, proposed by

Schleicher, between languages and living organisms; and there is a growing tendency to deplore the emphasis laid upon diachronic development at the expense of synchronic description.

Certainly in its traditional form the historical study of languages can hardly be considered as a branch of linguistics in the contemporary mode: it is concerned with the causal explanation of individual items—in fact with 'history in reverse'—rather than with the analysis of structure; it is positivist in assuming its facts to reside in the documents which form its material—its interest, as the late Viggo Brøndal expressed it, is in 'les petits faits vrais', whereas in linguistics, as in other branches of science, the contemporary attitude is anti-positivist.[1]

It is true that recent years have seen the brilliant synthesizing work of André Martinet in structural historical phonology; but here linguistic methods are imposed upon history, rather than the reverse, and time is but one dimension of the matrix in which the material is embedded. This view is confirmed by the experience of Jost Trier, in his work on the less frequented field of structural semantics, which led him to conclude that history conceived in structural terms must be a kind of comparative statics.[2] In fact, Martinet's fruitful theory of 'structural asymmetry' suggests the possibility of revising our ideas of linguistic 'explanation'; suppose, for example, that (as in Romance) a shift of velar to palatal articulation is accompanied by the shift of labiovelar to velar: in such a case one may say, in the familiar causal mode, that the delabialization (of e.g. k^w to k) is brought about by the palatalization (of e.g. k to $t\int$) —since it has created a gap in the velar position to which the labiovelar is attracted. But equally one may, with Trubetzkoy,

---

[1] *Acta Linguistica*, I. 1 (1939), p. 2.
[2] *Der deutsche Wortschatz im Sinnbezirk des Verstandes*, p. 13 (Ullmann, *The Principles of Semantics*, p. 167).

adopt the teleological metaphor[1] and say that the palatalization takes place to make way for the delabialization—in fact
that y IS y not only because it WAS x but also because it WILL
BE z. And one may come to the conclusion that either metaphor
is better avoided.

These remarks should not be taken to imply that diachronic
studies of the traditional type are to be discouraged or be-
littled: but the climate in which they prosper is historical
rather than linguistic. Nor is their preoccupation with documents any criticism in itself: the emphasis in linguistics is
admittedly upon spoken material, but one need not deny the
legitimacy of analysing written language in its own right—in
that case, however, the analyst should be honest, and (unless
the written language is otherwise unknown) should not work
with one eye upon a spoken language which his documents are
presumed to represent; if issues are not to be prejudged, the
investigation of the relationship between spoken and written
forms must come after the analysis of each.[2] If, on the other
hand, one seeks a phonological interpretation of written
material (as in the common case of a known dead language),
then the first step must be to convert the written sequences into
phonetic terms as specific as the evidence will permit, and then
to apply to the resulting data the analytical methods appropriate to the study of spoken language. One is otherwise in
danger of accepting the elements of the written text as phonological facts—whereas they represent at best an ancient and
often inadequate attempt at analysis.[3] There are no facts in
linguistics until the linguist has made them; they are ultimately,
like all scientific facts, the products of imagination and invention:[4] 'Experience by itself is "silent", and it requires a hypo-

[1] *Psychologie du Langage* (*Journal de Psychologie*, 30), p. 245.
[2] Cf. Angus McIntosh, 'The Analysis of Written Middle English', *Trans. Phil. Soc.*
1956.
[3] Cf. Allen, 'Phonetics and Comparative Linguistics', *Archivum Linguisticum*, III, 2.
[4] Cf. Woodger, *Biology and Language*, p. 61.

thesis in order to give it a voice. . . . Things, events, and facts do not speak, but the scientist does.'[1]

From this it is clear that the linguist, *qua* linguist, cannot be expected to share the philologist's enthusiasm for the discovery of ancient materials. His interest is in analysis rather than historical explanation; and there still remains a vast body of living material to engage his attention—material intact in all its fullness and complexity, as it proceeds from the mouths of its speakers and functions in its social context; he is therefore less attracted by the shadowy reflections of language which documents provide, particularly in those cases where the meanings and even the forms may be matters of controversy— the interest of such material for cryptanalysis and pre-history is of course another matter. Yet the traditions of philology have laid undue stress upon this kind of material; and warnings such as those of Schuchardt have gone too long unheeded:

'The present', he wrote, 'is more important for science than the past. For its purpose is to comprehend events, and in this it can best succeed if they are present to immediate observation. We can comprehend past events only by reference to the present: we have to "re-present" them to ourselves. As the movements of dunes and glaciers illuminate the pre-history of the earth's surface, so does our everyday speaking and hearing illuminate the prehistory of language';[2] yet, he continues, we

1 Hutten, *The Language of Modern Physics*, p. 224.
2 I take the opportunity of quoting, in the fullness they deserve, the words of Hermann Paul—himself an uncompromising protagonist of the historical method —which are as relevant today as when first expressed some seventy years ago: 'Dass es keine andere exakte Darstellung der Laute einer Sprache gibt, als diejenige, die uns lehrt, welche Organbewegungen erforderlich sind, um sie hervorzubringen, das bedarf heutzutage keines Beweises mehr. Das Ideal einer solchen Darstellungs- weise ist nur da annähernd zu erreichen, wo wir in der Lage sind, Beobachtungen an lebendigen Individuen zu machen. Wo wir nicht so glücklich sind, muss uns dies Ideal wenigstens immer vor Augen schweben, müssen wir uns bestreben, ihm so nahe als möglich zu kommen, aus dem Surrogate der Buchstabenschrift die

still have an unhealthy respect for the 'dead' languages—with the result that we come to set higher value upon a mutilated Apollo than upon an intact masterpiece.[1]

In a review by J. Z. Young of a recent biography of Darwin, the evolutional discovery is held at least partly responsible for biology being 'still a somewhat inexact science' some fifty years after the event. 'Darwin', he points out, 'was the simple naturalist, dissecting patiently, amassing facts over the years, knowing and caring little of philosophy.' Whilst one cannot but respect the Darwinian virtues in general, contemporary linguistics, in growing painfully out of the natural-history stage, can only find them constraining. It is perhaps no paradox to claim that the effects of certain material discoveries may in fact be to hinder the progress of a science, by distracting attention to the *use* of the new material, however fragmentary, and away from the invention of more adequate concepts for the *analysis* of what we already possess.

These remarks are offered with a full realization of the important part played by the so-called 'discovery' of Sanskrit, leading to the vigorous activity of nineteenth-century comparative philology; it was this atmosphere that fostered the interest and material endowments out of which the new linguistics has grown. The linguist is indeed grateful for such stimuli; but he continues to respect the Cartesian distinction of 'science' and 'connaissance',[2] and tenders his loyalty to the former: it is to be noted that Descartes himself classified the

lebendige Erscheinung, so gut es gehen will, herzustellen. Dies Bestreben kann aber nur demjenigen glücken, der einigermassen lautphysiologisch geschult ist, der bereits Beobachtungen an lebenden Sprachen gemacht hat, die er auf die toten übertragen kann, der sich ausserdem eine richtige Vorstellung über das Verhältnis von Sprache und Schrift gebildet hat. Es eröffnet sich also schon hier ein weites Feld für die Kombination, schon hier zeigt sich Vertrautheit mit den Lebensbedingungen des Objekts als notwendiges Erfordernis' (*Prinzipien der Sprachgeschichte*[5], p. 30).

[1] *Brevier*, pp. 332 f.

[2] Cf. *Oeuvres*, ed. Adam and Tannery, x, 502.

study of language together with history and geography as a 'connaissance'—but that he had practical knowledge rather than analysis in mind appears from the provocative remark ascribed to him by Vico, that 'to know Latin is to know no more than Cicero's servant-girl did'.[1]

I have suggested that linguistics is concerned primarily with the living utterance. Such an indication of one's subject-matter carries with it a presupposition—the basic presupposition of our study. We presume that there is a particular mode of human behaviour which it is legitimate to isolate and to label as 'language'; we assume also that this behaviour is such that systematic statements may be made about its various manifestations. It is probably the most 'systematizable' of all forms of overt behaviour, whence arises the greater rigour of linguistics compared with other social sciences. It follows naturally from this that the linguist tends primarily to be interested in those aspects of the subject which involve the highest degree of systematization—as, for example, phonology and grammar; it follows also that he is little concerned with an itemizing activity such as etymology; in the difficult field of semantics, theories of systematic statement are at an experimental stage. In Western linguistics over the last hundred years, the trend has been from the less to the more systematic studies; but, as a result of the persistence of popular superstition, the earlier, less systematic studies have come to be widely conceived as the prime occupation of the linguist: particularly is this the case with etymology, and particularly with that practice of it which has been termed 'the old curiosity-shop school of linguistics'.

This statement of a positive presupposition may be matched by an emphatic negation—which is, that linguistics assumes *no* categories *in rebus*, *no* system inherent in the material and

[1] Giambattista Vico, *Opere* (Laterza edn.), I, 274 [cf. also I, 35 f.]: see Fisch and Bergin (trsl.), *The Autobiography of G. Vico*, Introd. p. 37.

awaiting discovery. Linguistics, as I have already suggested, is a creative and not an observational activity: it creates its elements out of the continuum of human speech: it does not observe units unfolding themselves in time, but selects from the continuum such data as are relevant to the characterization of the elements it has established. It is true that some linguists would in fact assume the system to be immanent in the language, and the linguistic analysis to be a process of discovery rather than invention. They might also claim that in any case one's epistemological outlook makes no practical difference. But if a system is supposed to exist in reality, it is presumably a definite, single system; and the assumption of such a system rules out the possibility of alternative analyses. This seems a high price to pay for the satisfaction of presuming to deal in realities. The essential criteria for linguistic statement are generally agreed to comprise simplicity, exhaustiveness, and self-consistency; but it is usual to encounter some conflict between these requirements (more especially the first two), and the proportions of each may then be varied according to the predilections of the linguist and the particular purposes of his statement. We may recall a recently published note of de Saussure's, in which he says: 'This is our profession of faith in linguistics . . . that there are no given objects, no things which continue to exist when we pass from one conceptual framework to another.'[1]

There remains the question of method. It is a predominant feature of transatlantic linguistics that method is identified with procedure;[2] and there are important handbooks now in existence which lay down detailed operational techniques for linguistic analysis. In this country the tendency has been to eschew the assembly-line process, and to leave the application

---

[1] *Cahiers F. de Saussure*, 12, p. 58.
[2] See, however, C. Hockett, *Studies in Linguistics*, 7, p. 49.

of the theory to the genius of the individual craftsman. The stress is upon the prerequisite theory and the resultant statement, and these two are assessed without regard to the intervening processes: so far as method enters into our reckoning, it is to be identified with mode of statement. Such a lack of procedural postulates is not to be taken as a mark of weakness or disorganization: one may even argue that a crystallization of techniques—except for certain specifically organized projects—is liable to result in a fossilization of theory.

One result of the procedural approach is that the labour of analysis may be divided. Thus one worker, say a phonetically trained research student, may be sent into the field to collect and process the material by means of a phonemic technique—in the ambiguous words of a leading American phonetician, 'Phonetics gathers raw material. Phonemics cooks it.'[1] The resulting phonemic statement may then be taken over by another linguist, to provide the material for a morphemic and syntactical analysis of a hierarchically 'higher' order. And there is no doubt that the system works—it produces a means of writing, and a grammatical formulation: and a system of teaching geared to such techniques has shown impressive results. But it suffers from an inherent theoretical weakness, which can have practical repercussions; for any analysis involves a selection from the formless mass of phonic material; and if the phonetician does not know in advance the requirements of the grammarian, he cannot be sure what data most profitably to select or how best to process them;[2] whilst the grammarian cannot be certain that his analysis is the most appropriate to the material, without himself having examined that material phonetically. This vicious circle can be broken by the linguist himself alternating in the roles of phonetician

[1] Kenneth L. Pike, *Phonemics*, p. 57.
[2] Cf. Pike, 'Grammatical Prerequisites to Phonemic Analysis', *Word*, 3. 3, pp. 155 ff.

and grammarian, modifying his grammatical analysis as his phonetic investigations proceed, and guiding his phonetic inquiries by the progressive requirements of his grammar. This undoubtedly places a greater burden on the individual linguist, and compels even the most sublime to leave their ivory towers and struggle with the sometimes unpalatable complexities of 'uncooked' speech. The advantage of such an approach is that it leaves the way open for the linguist to decide, if he so wishes, that, for example, the phonemic theory itself is not entirely suitable for his particular grammatical statement, or even that phonological analysis is not a pre-prequisite to grammar: he may then process the material in terms of some other theory more fitted to his requirements.

If one cannot agree to lay down procedures for analysis, still less can one do so for the personal conduct of one's research in relation to native informants. The linguist is sometimes asked how he elicits his material: how does he guide his informant into the utterances which are crucial to his analysis? how does he effect the initial break-in to previously unknown material? Such matters I should prefer to regard as the individual's private and confidential business—they are irrelevant to his statement and it is the latter to which his activities are directed. It suffices to say that each linguist evolves his own techniques in accordance with his personality, with that of his informant, and with the social and personal relations obtaining between them. Many linguists, however, would probably agree that deception and ambush play an important part in producing the unselfconscious responses that are required; it is usually dangerous for the informant to know in detail what is wanted of him—he may oblige even if the material does not exist. It is true that the linguist's gospel comprises every word that proceeds from his informant's mouth—which cannot, by definition, be wrong; but it is no less true that, as a matter of principle, whatever the informant

18

volunteers *about* his language (as opposed to *in* it) must be assumed to be wrong—he is not after all a linguist (or if he is he will probably be a quite useless informant!); however, it is generally advisable to listen patiently and not to deprive him too sharply of his illusions—the good informant is a rare and valuable phenomenon, and his co-operation must be fostered with care.

My remarks thus far have had the object of delimiting in general the sphere of the linguistic discipline. I have now to mention certain particular trends which threaten to divert linguistic studies into non-linguistic channels.

Recent years have seen a movement in philosophy which has sometimes been known by the confusing title of 'linguistic analysis': its concern has been with the content-analysis of philosophical utterances, and so wide has been its influence that it might almost be said with Seneca, 'Quae philosophia fuit, facta philologia est.'

The method has typically involved the conversion of natural-language statements into presumed 'equivalent' forms such as would reveal their logical affinities.[1] It is at this point that the linguist feels uneasy: for the philosopher thereby begs the whole question of 'equivalence', which in the linguist's view, itself requires rigorous investigation. The point calls for notice, since similar methods are not entirely unknown even in linguistics: thus, in the famous work of Damourette and Pichon, we find the French negational statement '*non*' described as an 'abbreviated [sc. negative] representation of the preceding phrase': a linguist critic of this method has aptly described it as follows:

'One syntactical datum is replaced by something else which is said to "mean" the same thing, but which in fact represents another syntactical datum; then one analyses this second

[1] Cf. P. F. Strawson, 'Construction and Analysis', *The Revolution in Philosophy*, pp. 97 ff.

phenomenon, . . . and assumes that the first has thereby been analysed.'[1] Similar criticisms may be made of the procedure of 'catalysis' in glossematics;[2] and in philosophy itself Wittgenstein refers to such cases as when the abrupt command 'Slab!' is said to be an elliptical expression for 'Bring me a slab'. Why, says Wittgenstein, should one not equally say that 'Bring me a slab' is a lengthened form of 'Slab!'? 'And why', he goes on, 'should I translate the call "Slab!" into a different expression in order to say what someone means by it? Why should I not say "When he says 'Slab!' he means 'Slab!'"?'[3] This is precisely the linguistic point of view: for the linguist, in Wittgenstein's words, every sentence 'is in order as it is'. The linguist is concerned with the actual and not with the possible, with what is said, and not with what, according to the philosopher, might equally well have been said, but, owing to the perversity of natural language, was not.

Whilst the linguist must reject such methods in his own work, it is right that he should be aware of their existence in a neighbouring field. Would that the philosopher were more aware of the methods of linguistics: in a recent work entitled *The Revolution in Philosophy* we do indeed find a recognition that the analysis of natural language-structures may be of interest—but we find also a complete unawareness that such studies are already pursued (pp. 115 f.); the writer concludes by 'venturing the prediction that this little-trodden path will be trodden to some purpose before very long'.—As well might one hazard the revolutionary prophecy that steam might soon be harnessed for purposes of locomotion.

Whilst one aspect of philosophy offers some slight embarrassment on the one side, a more dangerous diversion has been

[1] C. de Boer, *'Innovations' en matière d'analyse linguistique* (*Med. d. Kon. Akad. v. Wetensch., Afd. Letterkunde, Deel* 79, *Serie A, No.* 1), p. 15.
[2] Cf. Hjelmslev, *Prolegomena*, pp. 60 f.   [3] *Philosophical Investigations*, pp. 8 f.

created on the other by the concepts and techniques of communication engineering. A number of linguists have in fact accepted the validity of communicational criteria in linguistic studies—thereby perhaps reflecting the traditional body-and-soul metaphor of language as a vehicle for the communication of thought. An alternative view is that these criteria are appropriate to communicational studies, *and no more*. Perhaps the most crucial problem in this respect concerns the concept of 'redundancy'. From the standpoint of message-transmission, it is clearly uneconomical to send the same information twice, or to send it in a more complex form than is essential to its distinctiveness. Thus, in a language which exhibits the common phenomenon generally known as 'vowel-harmony', the presence of a front vowel in the initial syllable of a word might involve fronted varieties of vowel in succeeding syllables; it would therefore be redundant, from the communicational point of view, to transmit the information 'frontness' in respect of other than the first syllable. And if, as in English, all nasal articulations are voiced, it is redundant to transmit voice as well as nasality. All languages abound in such so-called redundancies; as was stated at a Speech Communication Conference at the Massachusetts Institute of Technology in 1950: 'Speech communication is relatively inefficient compared to an ideal sending and receiving system using the same sound spectrum.'[1]

In accordance with such observations there has been a tendency for linguists to describe their material in similar terms.[2] This might be interpreted as arguing a misunderstanding of the true function of linguistics. If it is in the nature of language to be of such a character as has been described, it is the function of the linguist to analyse and state it in its own characteristic terms, and not to ascribe to it superfluities which are such only by reference to other and irrelevant

---

[1] *Journal of the Acoustical Society of America*, 22. 6, p. 690.
[2] Cf. Jakobson, Fant and Halle, *Preliminaries to Speech Analysis*, esp. pp. 44 f.

criteria. In phonology, the analysis in terms of redundancy is largely encouraged by the linearity of roman transcription, which demands the localization of certain features (e.g. 'frontness') in a particular sequential 'segment' or 'letter', when they might more appropriately be considered as properties of a larger unit such as the word. Techniques for non-linear, multidimensional statement are now at an active stage of development.[1]

A further disquieting trend originates within linguistics itself; I refer to the denial, in certain quarters, of the relevance of meaning to linguistic analysis. This attitude is in some ways understandable, since meaning has long been one of the least satisfactory aspects of linguistic studies; it has been dominated by the dualism of content and expression, and subservient to changing fashions in psychology—to the theories of Durkheim under de Saussure, and to Weissian behaviourism under Bloomfield. Meaning, as at least one linguist has expressed it, has become 'a dirty word'; but if the name tends to be avoided, there is no doubt that every linguist employs the concept, though some would be unwilling to admit to such improper thoughts. And surely without meaning linguistics cannot exist.

It has been remarked that 'linguistics is peculiar among mathematical systems in that it abuts upon reality in two places instead of one'.[2] I should not wish to stress the idea of linguistics as a form of mathematics—although its effective operation certainly demands the use of quasi-algebraic modes of expression, and it is likely that some future developments will require an understanding of statistical techniques. It is certainly a subject not inimical to the mathematical mind—

[1] Cf. with reference to 'vowel-harmony' (in *Bull. Sch. Or. & Afr. St.* XVIII. 3, 1956), N. Waterson, 'Some Aspects of the Phonology of the Nominal Forms of the Turkish Word' (pp. 578 ff.); F. R. Palmer, ' "Openness" in Tigre: a Problem in Prosodic Statement' (pp. 561 ff.).

[2] M. Joos, *J. Acoust. Soc. Am.* 22. 6, p. 701.

one may mention the name of Grassmann, or of our own Joseph Wright, who said, 'Everybody who would be a philologist must have done mathematics or be capable of doing mathematics';[1] whilst Pāṇini, the incomparable Indian grammarian, was employing the concept of zero for linguistic purposes many centuries before its appearance in mathematics.[2]

But, reverting to the position of linguistics, it is true that it is peculiar amongst sciences in standing astride two streams of phenomena—on one side the phonic material which constitutes speech, and on the other the practical situations in which speech operates. These situations or 'contexts' may be considered as functions of the phonic material which operates within them, or in other words as the 'meanings' of that material.[3]

We could no doubt analyse the material without reference to meaning, but then the theory governing the analysis would have to be determined by some other subject, such as acoustics or physiology. And from either of these standpoints speech would probably not turn out to be particularly interesting material: more interesting noises could be found for acoustic analysis, and more interesting bodily activities for physiological analysis. It is only when we analyse phonic material by reference to its contextual function that those peculiarly systematic statements become possible which are characteristic of linguistics. An analysis which ignored such function, and concerned itself solely with the phonic material, might, for example, define its units in terms of arbitrary vocal intervals and the pauses between them; for linguistics, as Professor Bazell has observed, 'the unit so defined would have the interesting property that nothing whatever profitable could be said about

---

[1] E. M. Wright, *The Life of Joseph Wright*, I, p. 74.
[2] Cf. my 'Zero and Pāṇini', *Indian Linguistics*, 16 (Chatterji Jubilee vol.), pp. 106 ff.
[3] Cf. Firth, 'The Technique of Semantics', *T.P.S.* 1935.

it'[1]—it may be mentioned that the authors of one such study, undertaken for entirely non-linguistic purposes,[2] refrain from giving their unit a linguistic name such as 'sentence', 'phrase', or 'clause', and christen it 'talk-spurt'. The only reason for distinguishing any two sets of phonic data as *linguistically* different is the fact that their functions are different: there is no *a priori* reason why one should consider the difference between the r and l sounds in English to be such as to justify their allotment to different phonological units; what does justify such an allotment is their consistently distinctive function in regard to the contexts in which they occur. r is different from l because, *inter alia*, a ram is different from a lamb; and z is different from d because, *inter alia*, has is not the same as had. We do not recognize phonic differences if they do not have different semantic functions—nor, it may be added, semantic differences if they do not involve phonic differences. This may be made clear if one sets out a general conspectus of theory.

Our material, as we have seen, consists on the one side of *phonic* events, and on the other of *situational* events (which may include, or even entirely consist of, other phonic events than those which are in the focus of present attention). The discipline of *phonetics* provides the tools for the analysis of phonic events, and by their means particular data are selected for the establishment of formal categories; according to the kind of criteria involved in the selection, such categories are said to be *phonological* or *grammatical*—phonological if they are based primarily upon similarities or dissimilarities of phonic data and secondarily upon their combinative relations: and grammatical if the converse is the case.[3] The phonetic analysis is

---

[1] *Word*, 8. 1, p. 35.

[2] Norwine and Murphy, 'Characteristic Time Intervals in Telephonic Conversation', *Bell Syst. Tech. Pub.* Monog. B–1074 (=*B.S.T.J.* 17, 281 ff.).

[3] Cf. Bazell, *Linguistic Form* (Istanbul, 1953), p. 18.

not necessarily congruent with that of acoustics ('sibilant', for example, seems to have no clear acoustic correlate), or with that of physiology (thus the 'blade of the tongue' is not an anatomically relevant abstraction). On the other side, *semantics* provides the tools for the analysis of situational events; this analysis likewise is not necessarily congruent with that of logic, psychology, sociology, or even common sense: it is simply such analysis as permits the most fruitful phonetic analysis to be made.

The actual procedure is in fact to seek differences in the phonic material and to provide support for them from the situational; the phonetic discipline is consequently more highly organized than the semantic, which remains rather on an *ad hoc* basis. It is possible to imagine a linguistics in which the emphasis would be reversed—in which one noted primarily differences in situations, and supported these by differences in phonic events: two situations would then be different only if they involved differences in phonic events—a ram would be different from a lamb only because r differed from l, and present would be different from past because, *inter alia*, the z of has differed from the d of had. But the procedure actually adopted is determined by factors of economy; the phonic elements are generally more limited both in extent and inventory than the situational; and whilst phonic events invariably occur within a situational context, many situational events have no phonic ingredients. But it is only by the interlocking roles of the two analyses that our categories are guaranteed their linguistic status.

I conclude by considering a not infrequent criticism of contemporary linguistic method, namely that its results may leave the reader with the feeling 'that we have come by devious and rather tedious ways to something which looks suspiciously like the old grammar'. Whilst such an observation can hardly be extended to phonology, it has perhaps some justification in the grammatical field, so far as it concerns the classical languages and to a lesser extent the Indo-European languages in general. This situation arises because of a certain parallelism between grammatical distinctions and situational distinctions viewed from a commonsense or logical standpoint (I shall not enter into the controversy concerning how far these views in their turn are coloured by the grammatical structure of the viewer's native language). The traditional grammatical statements have been arrived at largely by non-grammatical, situational criteria, whereas the contemporary method will have formulated its grammatical statements by reference to grammatical criteria. If the two statements to some extent coincide, that is interesting, but it neither justifies the former nor invalidates the latter. It is possible to arrive at the right solution by the wrong means, or without knowing how one arrived there.

The achievements of contemporary linguistics may not yet appear particularly impressive—but at least it is capable of defining its concepts and of stating the criteria upon which its results are based. If its theory seems at times to be in advance of its practice, that is a healthy symptom.

Linguistic Typology

An inaugural lecture delivered on 26 February 1958 by
C. E. BAZELL, *Professor of General Linguistics in the University of London*

Linguistic Typology

Author's Note
This lecture, which of course was not addressed to specialists, concerns mainly the widely popularized 'morphological' typology.

The insistence on the legitimacy of mere differences of taste in linguistic description was made in a climate very different from that of today. Then, one linguist could accuse another of a grave blunder for having taken English to have a singular zero-morpheme in the noun; now, the same linguist would be pleading for the 'tolerance' of various alternative descriptions alongside each other even when one may be clearly better than the rest.

However the clear superiority of one model over another, now amply demonstrated for higher-level syntax, is less acceptable in morphology. It does not seem to make much difference whether one takes English to have a singular morpheme, or merely to have a form of the noun which lacks the plural morpheme, from the standpoint of the system as a whole.

Yet such small matters may prove crucial in a morphological typology. Thus Emmon Bach's statement that 'purely isolating and purely agglutinative languages would presumably differ from fusional languages by having no rules of the form "x + y→z"', while presupposing the plausibility of the traditional classification, hardly makes sense if these small matters are not to play an essential role.

For instance, if Finnish is taken to have 'nominative' and 'singular' morphemes, then the Finnish plural suffix -*t* will be accounted for by a rule of this form: Nom. + Plural.→-*t*. If, however, the traditional nominative case and singular number are regarded respectively as the mere absence of case and number, the plural will not be derived 'fusionally', but rather by a rule

$$\text{Plural ( )} \rightarrow \text{-}t$$

which may be read as 'the plural is represented as -*t* when no case-morpheme follows', or (the same thing) 'when the plural morpheme is word-terminal'.

This seems a more appropriate kind of solution at least for a language like Turkish; but R. B. Lees, who gives us separate 'nominative' and 'singular' morphemes (ultimately reduced to

29

zero) in respect of the Turkish noun, can undoubtedly claim that his analysis is, in some respects, more simple. At the cost of a few additional symbols, all forms of the Turkish noun (or at least those which enter into phrase-structure) are generated by rules of equal complexity, and are parallel in structure. This puts in second place the number of symbol-tokens as a criterion. Now Sydney Lamb, while appearing to accept this criterion, accuses the transformational grammarians of representing their systems as simpler than they really are, by failing to count essential though covert symbols. His specific objection is that a series of *ordered* rules is more complex than a set of rules that can be applied in any order, since in the former case the number of the rule must be reckoned as an additional symbol.

While it is possible to argue about the status of rule-numberings, which seem intermediate between symbols of the grammar and symbols of the meta-theory, the real difference between Lamb and the transformationalists would appear to be one of aesthetics. Ordered rules (provided that the ordering is not arbitrary) are more pleasing than unordered rules, and for linguists who feel this, any criterion of simplicity weighted against ordered rules is in so far void. Lamb evidently does not feel this. While it is impossible to say with confidence that such a difference could never become the subject of rational argument, it does not seem likely that it could.

My remarks in this inaugural lecture were widely interpreted as the statement of a very popular view, namely that (i) inflectional languages are characterized by indeterminacy of segments (ii) isolating languages by indeterminacy of classes, while (iii) agglutinative languages are free of either indeterminacy.

I did not try to defend this popular but erroneous view. The non-minimal morphological segments of 'inflectional languages' represented by the *words* of traditional grammar make a quite unusually well-defined class of segments. The indeterminacy of classes in 'isolating languages' is no more than a popular myth, as is equally the idea that 'agglutinative languages' present exceptionally determinate systems.

What does differentiate the three traditional types of language is the *locus* of indeterminacy. It is characteristic of inflectional languages that the smallest determinate morphological segments (roughly 'words') are syntactically very complex. It is characteristic of isolating languages that the members of the small-est determinate morphological classes may be segmentally very complex. The simplest segments do not fall as such into syntactic classes, much as the simplest classes in inflectional languages do not correspond to classes of segments, in any direct way.

Agglutinative languages enjoy no priority over others in respect of determinacy. In such languages there is indeed, according to all grammatical descriptions, a close correspondence between morphemes and morphs—between these classes and their repre-sentative segments. But two different structural accounts of the Turkish noun will provide respectively for one or five morphemes in the same 'word' and correspondingly for one or five morphs. What characterizes a language like Turkish is by no means a greater determinacy, but rather the absence of any conflict between classification and segmentation. Morphemes and morphs are selected simultaneously, but the selection itself may be far more dubious than in the supposedly 'less determinate' systems of other language-types.

Within the domain of syntax, it is plausibly assumed that phrase-structure rules are very similar in all natural languages, whereas transformational rules differ widely. This is an old insight: it was always recognized that the so-called 'structural order' of units in German is very different from their linear order, and very similar to the order (both structural *and linear*) of units in Turkish. Recent work on German (e.g. the book of Bierwisch on the German verb-phrase) is confirmatory. The 'linearity' of Turkish consists in the relatively few transformations needed to derive the surface-structure from the depth-structure.

If this is so, then there is an optimal point in a grammar for the application of typology. Typology is not very profitable in the domain of phrase-structure, since languages do not differ much in interesting ways. It is very profitable in the domain of transformation. It is less profitable again in the domain of morphology, not because languages do not differ but rather because the *locus* of the difference tends to be more obscure. Finally, phonological typology cannot even be given the informal status I have granted to morphological typology in this lecture.

Linguistic Typology, understood as the classification of langu-ages according to their general structure rather than according to their historical or geographical relationship, has never been a favourite topic among professional linguists, though the reasons for this have varied. Before the late nineteenth century, the material for such a study barely existed, and by that time most scholars were more profitably engaged in historical linguistics and what is still called 'comparative philology'. The attention now given to the synchronic analysis of individual languages has led us to revise our ideas about what the comparative philologists were really doing: it is no longer uncritically accepted that they were restoring lost stages of linguistic development in quite the way that they themselves supposed.[1] But if the subject has changed, the subject-matter remains the same: comparison is between those languages which would hitherto have been referred, without much hesitation, to a common 'parent-language'. To this form of comparative study has been added the study of structural affinities between languages geographically contiguous though perhaps genetically unrelated.[2] Yet it remains true that typologies based purely on general structure tend to be regarded with the same suspicion as before.

One reason for this is that while linguists have come to treat the structure of an individual language as having importance quite independently of its predecessors or other related languages, they have also come to see that this structure is not something given in the language, but that it has to be 'analysed out' of the material by the linguist, and that if one linguist differs in his analysis from the other it does not follow that either he or the other linguist is wrong. Of course there may be logical inconsistencies, errors due to mere ignorance, and divergences fairly attributable to sheer perversity on the part of one analyst. But there are few scholars left who would be inclined to refer most differences in the analysis of a language to one of these

[1] Cf. W. S. Allen, 'Relationship in Comparative Linguistics', *T.P.S.* 1953.
[2] Cf. R. Jakobson, 'Über die phonologischen Sprachbünde', *T.C.L.P.* iv.

three sources. Differences in description may be legitimate differences, not to be resolved by further information, logical argument, or an appeal to common sense. Now this is not felt as a grave inconvenience in the usual comparative studies, since it suffices there that linguists recognize, in each other's analyses, some plausible connexion between the description and the material. It is open to the linguist, providing he does not pass beyond this point of recognition, to give just such analyses of the different languages concerned, or rather of partial systems of these languages, as will throw into relief the relations he wishes to show. The same is true when he is concerned to demonstrate structural affinities in a geographic group. But this sort of partiality, which is not merely excusable but is rather a necessity where the subject is a particular set of languages, seems quite out of place in a *general* typology. Hence the demand, whenever the question of structural typology arises, for neutral descriptions based on agreed criteria, identical from linguist to linguist and from the description of one language to that of all others. Such a demand is surely preposterous, and if linguistic typology depends on its satisfaction the subject had better be abandoned forthwith.

Another reason why a general typology might appear infeasible is that languages do not present homogeneous systems, but rather sets of overlapping systems, and therefore it is at best these, rather than languages as a whole, which would be the material for a typology. The monosystemic analysis still favoured in some circles is yielding ground to the polysystemic type of analysis advocated especially by Professor J. R. Firth.[1] However, it may still be possible to recognize nuclear or dominant types, at least in favourable cases. If we shall speak here for simplicity's sake of 'language-types', this must not be understood to imply that even the languages chosen as model cases present the characteristic type throughout.

[1] Cf. J. R. Firth, 'Sounds and Prosodies', *T.P.S.* 1948.

However, before arguing (as I am going to) that there is at least one possible form of general typology, I should like to stress that I do not believe that *all* linguistic levels are favourable to some form of typology. Phonology, for instance, would seem a most unfavourable domain. For here linguists tend to diverge in their criteria of relevance, so that a feature which is present in the material for one is for the other virtually non-existent. Happily, in the morphological domain the divergences are not of the same kind: the different descriptions have a recognizable common basis. This is illustrated by the fact that many morphologists are ready to avail themselves of traditional orthography (where it exists) in the citation of forms; the reader is supposed to supply his own phonological analysis of the forms cited, and it is assumed that it does not matter, from the morphological standpoint, what kind of phonological analysis he adopts. Admittedly this practice breaks down over some disputed features such as stress and juncture; but the overall picture is that of scholars discussing the treatment of a common material, not, as with phonology, of scholars in strife over what the material is, or should be.

Now this 'common material', while affording a basis for a morphological typology, still cannot justify the sort of typology which operates with specific linguistic units. The two most recent proposals, by Professor Knud Togeby[1] and Professor Joseph Greenberg,[2] are of this sort. Togeby sets up a scheme involving such categories as case and mood, and languages are allotted their position in the scheme according to whether they possess, or lack, certain of these categories. Greenberg seeks

[1] K. Togeby, 'Structure immanente de la langue française', *T.C.L.C.* vi.
[2] J. H. Greenberg, 'A Quantitative Approach to the Morphological Typology of Language', in *Method and Perspective in Anthropology* (Papers in honour of Wilson D. Wallis, Minneapolis, 1953). Greenberg's definitions leave a very wide scope indeed for different interpretations: for instance, it is only from a footnote on p. 210 that one may guess that Greenberg favours 'zero elements' of the kinds discussed below.

greater generality, by operating only with such terms as *word*, *morpheme*, and *morph*. The word was, of course, the basic unit in the older typologies.

Now there is perhaps no unit over which there is less agreement than the word. If there is any agreement at all, it is that the word has to be differently defined for each language analysed, and that there is at best a kind of 'family resemblance' between the different uses of the term. In this respect the *word* is on a par with such specific categories as *case* or *mood*. Only in practice the difference in application goes still further. We shall have occasion to cite from English an instance in which one linguist would reckon with a single word where most others would speak of four or five separate words. For several languages of south-east Asia, e.g. Vietnamese, linguists hesitate whether to identify the word with the minimal morphological segment, which here is taken to coincide with the syllable, or with clusters of such segments.[1] For Chinese, the typical 'isolating' language of traditional typology, the position is more complicated: most linguists refuse to identify 'word' and 'minimal segment' so far at least as the *modern* language is concerned,[2] but some deny the applicability of the term at all.[3] It would be easy to say that these linguists are merely using the term *word* in quite different senses. We shall see that it is not as simple as this.

In illustration of the way in which analyses of the same speech data may differ, examples from the domains of morphological classification and morphological segmentation, the former from English and the latter from Latin, may serve.

Traditional grammars have it that many English words can

[1] For the former view cf. M. B. Emeneau, *Studies in Vietnamese Grammar*, 1951, p. 44; and for the latter P. J. Honey, 'Word Classes in Vietnamese', *B.S.O.A.S.* xviii.

[2] Cf. M. A. K. Halliday, 'Grammatical Categories in Chinese', *T.P.S.* 1956; H. F. Simon, 'Two Substantival Complexes in Standard Chinese', *B.S.O.A.S.* xv.

[3] Cf. C. F. Hockett, *Language*, 20, p. 255.

be used both as nouns and as verbs—e.g. *call, stay, seal, show,* &c. This is one way of putting the position. But the linguist has many ways open to him of stating it.

One linguist will state that there is a relation of overlapping between the classes of noun and verb, such that the same unit may be a member of both classes.

A second linguist may state that there are three classes of unit here, three parts of speech (if he uses this term), the functional range of one class covering the functional range of the other two combined. So if we choose to call *thief* a noun, and *rob* a verb, we shall have to find a third term for such units as *call* and *show.*

By a third linguist, *call* and *show* might be taken as different units, mere homophones, in one function and the other. As with the second linguist, there would be no overlapping of classes, though there would be an overlapping of *forms* from one class to the other.

A fourth linguist might choose to say that there is only one class of words here, containing, however, a fair number of words with defective paradigms: from his standpoint, the absence of *virtued** or *he virtues** from the paradigm of *virtue* would be on a par with the absence of *an oat** or *a tong** from the paradigm of *oats* and *tongs.*

If each of these four linguists took his system seriously from the standpoint of typology, the first would say that English has a large measure of overlapping in its categories; the second that not the categories, but rather their ranges, overlap; the third that English is characterized by a large number of homonyms; and finally the fourth, that it is characterized by a large number of defective paradigms.

We are assuming that the four linguists, while differing so strongly over classification, are in agreement on morphological segmentation; that they do not differ by allotting different parts of the word to stem *vis-à-vis* inflexion. (Though, if phonologists, they will certainly have deviant analyses of the minor segmentation.)

A Latin noun-form such as *puellārum* may be segmented by an analyst in such ways as the following: stem *puell-*, termination *-ārum*; stem *puellā-*, termination *-rum;* stem *puellă-*, termination *-rum* with lengthening of stem-vowel; or again *puell-*, *-ā-*, *-rum* in three segments. Many traditional Latin grammars tend to imply diverse contradictory segmentations at the same time; for instance, they call *puella* an *a*-stem, implying a segmentation *puellā-rum*, but in the paradigm make a graphic segmentation *puell-ārum*.

However, the divergent analyses of different linguists are not a fatal bar to a typology which, in rough outline, might be shared by all. For one can classify languages precisely according to the problems of analysis which each presents. During the past twenty years linguistic journals have been full of articles discussing the terms in which declensional and conjugational forms of Indo-European languages may best be segmented. Such discussions have not arisen over such languages as Chinese and Vietnamese. 'Well, of course not,' many may be tempted to say, 'every schoolboy knows that Chinese is a language without nominal or verbal paradigms.' But this is to put things the wrong way round. Paradigms are not given in a language, they are set up by linguists, in answer to a problem. Latin sets a problem of segmentation, since while it is easy to agree on such classes as 'noun', 'genitive', and 'plural'—the labels themselves, of course, are arbitrary—it is often difficult to find a determinate set of segments answering to these classes. Let us leave aside the notorious example of the cases and numbers, for which it is agreed that no corresponding segments can be found. It remains true that segments can be found to answer to the class of stems on the one hand and to that of inflexions on the other, but just where to segment is a problem on which linguists are divided against each other or even against themselves.

37

The paradigms found in traditional Latin grammars are a sort of solution to the problem: they show the class-relations but do not tell one where to segment. The refusal to analyse in terms of segments is one answer to the problem of segmentation.

But with such languages as Chinese and Vietnamese this problem does not arise. Scholars are, in general, agreed on the minimal morphological segments: the question is rather, how to classify them by distribution. It is a problem of classes, not of segments. (By classes, I shall always understand *distributional* classes; 'synthetic' rather than 'analytic' classes in the sense of Mr W. Haas.)[1] And one answer to this problem is a refusal to analyse in terms of classes. But, of course, the fact that there are agreed minimal segments is an invitation to classifiy them, just as the fact that in Indo-European languages there are agreed minimal classes is an invitation to find corresponding segments where feasible. Hence the discussions of Chinese scholars on how the minimal segments can be classified, as well as whether they can feasibly be classified (though all these scholars agree roughly on what are the *segments* in question); answering to the discussions of European scholars on how the minimal classes can best be given segmental equivalents (though all these scholars agree roughly on what are the *classes* in question). Of course, both segmentation and classification must be made somewhere. But the Chinese scholar may choose to leave classification to a higher level, to classify rather only clusters of segments (with single segments, when they fit into such classification, as degenerate instances of clusters); while the Latin scholar may choose to segment into larger units only, roughly answering to 'words' in his description. Indeed the 'word' might be defined, for Latin, as the lowest level of determinate segmentation.

The usual way of characterizing Chinese as representative of its type is to say that its words are of one segment only. This

[1] W. Haas, 'On Defining Linguistic Units', *T.P.S.* 1954.

will simply not fit most modern descriptions, which abandon the tradition of equating the number of words with the number of written characters. Nor do all linguists find it useful to use the term *word* at all in their descriptions.

Another way of making the characterization is to say that the language lacks inflexions. But we can best see what use a term like *inflexion* has in connexion with another language-type.

The third of the traditional three types was the agglutinative, of which Turkish was cited as the model example. This model example, at least, fits the third possibility left along the dimension under discussion: namely a language for which segmentation and classification tend to become determinate *simultaneously*. In other words our minimal determinate classes will be classes of minimal determinate segments. We then have three types: (i) represented by Latin, for which linguists can match their classes before they can match their segments; (ii) represented by Chinese or better Vietnamese, for which they can match their segments before they can match their classes; and (iii) represented by Turkish, for which they can match their classes and segments at the same point.

Now Turkish is said to have *inflexions*, though by a strange terminological inconsistency it is contrasted as agglutinative with the inflexional languages in the narrower sense. However, it is very doubtful whether the distinction of derivational affix, inflexion, and independent particle would have been set up for Turkish if the model of Indo-European languages had been lacking. The distinction between inflexion and particle loses much of its point when, as here, both are equally identifiable as separate segments; and the distinction between derivational affix and inflexion loses much of its point when, as here, the boundaries between the two are so ill defined. It does not completely lose its point, and hence one cannot convict the authors of the descriptions of being unduly under the influence of Indo-European. But at least it is an open question whether the distinction is worth making. And when some of the reasons for making a distinction are lacking, the terms cannot be held equivalent to the same terms used in a description based on all these reasons. What applies to such terms as *inflexion* applies, of course, with equal or greater strength to more specific grammatical terms, such as *case* or *tense, genitive* or *perfect, noun* or *verb*.

An approach in terms of problems rather than of solutions renders us independent of the kind of analysis adopted for individual languages. Linguists can at least agree on such quasi-logical, pre-linguistic terms as *class* and *segment*. We are not, of course, relying on their ability to *apply* these terms in the same way. On the contrary, their ability to agree over the applications is made a *test* of the language type. We ask, in reference to the individual language, whether there are units which can be matched from one description to another, and whether these units are classes or segments. In other words, we ask *not* in what *determinate* way morphological segmentation and classification apply to this or that language. We ask more primitive questions: *whether* segmentation or classification apply in a determinate way, and, at whatever stage they do, whether this stage comes earlier for classes or for segments.

Many terms which are too ill defined to serve in a typology of systems can readily be accommodated in a problem typology. For instance the *word*.[1] Though linguists are not agreed on the operations which should lead to word-division, they all face in principle the same problem. It is a question of finding a well-characterized class of segments above the class of simple segments, suitable as a framework both for phonological and for syntactic statements. Trouble arises when no unit can be

---

[1] On the determinacy or indeterminacy of word-boundaries as a typological criterion, cf. P. Garvin, 'On the Relative Tractability of Morphological Data', *Word*, 13, and the present lecturer's review (*Istanbul Kültür Mecmuasi*, 1945) of V. Skalička, 'Über die Typologie der Bantusprachen', *Archiv Orientální*, xv.

found to fit both sorts of statement. Bloomfield was worried about the analysis of a group such as *the King of Norway's son*, where in phonological terms *Norway's* appears as a unit-word, while in syntactical terms the genitive belongs, not to *Norway*, but to *the King of Norway*. He proposed to solve the problem by calling *King of Norway's* a 'group-word'—which is a way of saying that it is like a group of words in one way but like a simple word in another. Another American linguist[1] chooses to call the 'genitive suffix' a 'clitic', by which he means that it is neither part of a word nor a word by itself; this is in contradiction to the normal demand that a sentence be divisible without residue into words. It would not I think be difficult to formulate the problem confronting the different linguists in a way which both would recognize as *his* problem, and without using terms like 'genitive' or 'noun-group' which may presuppose a particular analysis. And one can then ask whether a particular language tends to present this sort of problem.

It was assumed above that linguists can at least agree on whether a problem is a class-problem or a segment-problem. This does not imply that borderline cases may not arise. The following, for instance, is a class-segment problem:

In many languages of the type called 'agglutinative' by earlier typologists, every 'sign-segment' *either* may occur initally *or* may occur finally. At least this is the usual analysis.

English is roughly in this position, though it is not a striking example—e.g. in *bakers*, the element *-s* may occur finally (as it does here), the element *-er* (as in *baker*), and the element *bake* itself.

Now owing to the contrast between *baker* and *bakers*, and in order, so to speak, to *equalize* the elements in contrast, some linguists say that *baker* and *baker-s* do not differ by the number of their elements—if *bakers* has an 'inflexion' *-s*, then so has *baker* an inflexion—*zero*.

[1] K. L. Pike, 'A Problem in Morphology-Syntax Division', *Acta Linguistica*, v.

In the analysis of the traditional 'agglutinative language' *par excellence*, namely Turkish, which has a large number of elements comparable to the plural *-s* of *baker-s*, this method leads to a host of *zero-inflexions*, most of which bear such innocent labels as 'nominative', 'singular', 'indicative', 'third person', and so on.[1] However, there is a notable paradigm with no zero—namely, the personal possessive suffixes of the noun. Here there are first-, second-, and third-person suffixes, but no scholar has proposed a zero-suffix for the noun lacking an ostensive personal suffix. It is no good saying that, after all, the absence of a suffix *here* is quite simply its absence: the absence, namely, of person. This begs the question, which is precisely whether the so-called singular zero-suffix is not just the absence of number. One suspects that the peculiar treatment of the category of nominal person is due to the fact that no personal suffixes can be set up for the noun in the most familiar Indo-European languages. Had there existed here such a nominal category, and had the 'absence of person' had a positive exponent, this would have had a label; and then this label would quite happily have been applied to the Turkish forms. Since no linguist now would deliberately make one linguistic system the measure of another, differences of this sort can be resolved by rational argument.

Indeed it seems altogether probable that many linguists, faced with the consequences of applying their criteria consistently in this case, would simply revise their criteria so as to abandon, for Turkish, the host of zero-signs. But so far as the typologist is concerned, they would be welcome to stick to their criteria and apply them to the bitter end. For all differences which are not based on inconsistencies of application may be said to reflect an asymmetry in the basic material for analysis: which in the present context is not the *raw* material, but rather

[1] Cf. D. L. Olmsted 'Covert (or Zero) Morphemes and Morphemic Junction', *I.J.A.L.* 17.

the *common* material of the different analyses, defined through its recognition by all linguists seeking to justify these analyses.

The particular asymmetry in question is that of the positive and negative poles of inflexional oppositions—though for the purpose of simplicity we are going much beyond the bounds of the 'common material' in so phrasing it. The negative pole has no expression, as some scholars would put it. We may restore the symmetry by saying that it *has* an expression—*zero*. There is then a new asymmetry—that between the different sorts of phonological content of the two 'expressions'.

This example is on the borderline of segmental analysis and class analysis, since here it is the setting up of a class which is held to involve the setting up of a segment. Without a class of nominatives, there is no segment to be dealt with. Having created the class, the analyst looks round for its exponent.

I wish now to return to the example of the English verb and noun classes, in order to illustrate some of the ways in which I have given an over-simplified picture.

First, I assumed that the different analyses referred in some reasonable sense to the *same* segments, not that these segments would be given the same phonological analysis, but that, as *wholes*, they could be matched together in the different classifications. This is true, at best, only of the *productive* types in English. Another assumption, not stated, was that, though the classes of the different analysts were all different, the total sum of the segments in question was the same for all four: for instance, that one would not find, in the classification of one linguist, segments that could not even be said to overlap with segments in another classification. To express this in the terms of traditional grammar, we were assuming that none of the grammarians wanted to include among the words to be classified any that the others would have placed outside the noun-verb range and have called, e.g. adverbs. And to give an instance of what may happen, we may recall that one American linguist wished to class *better* in 'you better go' among the auxiliary verbs, like can in 'you can go'.[1]

This shows how hopeless it would be to ask for the 'most normal analysis' of English units in question, and to say: 'Most linguists deal with the units in this way, and we will classify English according to the majority opinion in respect of the noun-verb domain.' For the domain itself is not circumscribed. The indeterminacies cannot be given a determinate range to display themselves in.

But are the problems themselves any more determinate? I may have spoken as though one could say just what the question was that all the four imaginary linguists were solving in their own way. I should rather have said, that it would be possible to give a *model* of the question, perhaps in terms of some artificially constructed language, perhaps in terms of some more favourable actual language. Such terms as 'noun' and 'verb' would have no place in the model. Should we not find linguists in agreement about the nature of the question, and just for this reason in the *same* disagreement about the way of dealing with it? Or if not, could not at least one of them be convicted of inconsistency?

But when I speak of inconsistency, I do not suggest that there is any infallible way of cornering one's opponent in matters of grammatical analysis. When a little while ago I presumed to accuse of inconsistency those students of Turkish who set up a zero-case and a zero-number, without setting up a zero-person, I might have forgotten (though in fact I did not) a possible line of defence for them. They might have said: 'Having set up three persons for our verb, and even you will agree that this is reasonable, we chose to have the same number of persons for our noun. Of course, if we had considered the noun in isolation, we should have thought of your objection— and perhaps we would then have set up a fourth person. But

[1] Cf. B. Bloch, 'English Verb Inflection', *Language*, 23.

we began from a different end, and (much as we appreciate the point you've made) we stick to our own analysis.'

There are no doubt certain characteristic relations between class and segment which are likely to appear in almost all linguists' descriptions of a given language. In descriptions of Latin we find it common that the intersection of two classes does not answer to the conjunction of two segments: e.g. the intersection of 'genitive' and 'plural' does not answer to the conjunction of two segments as in the case of English *oxen's*, where the intersection of plural and genitive classes answers to the conjunction of the two segments -*n*- and -*z*. Whereas, in descriptions of Chinese, we shall more often find that the conjunction of two segments does not answer to the intersection of two classes.

However, this may be regarded as the limiting-case of the indeterminacy discussed above. When linguists often disagree over segmentation, there will be cases where they can most of of them agree not to segment at all. But it is easy to see these cases as termini, so to speak, of their respective problem-clusters.

The failure of linguists to match their descriptions may be due to a fundamental indeterminacy, such as cannot be re-solved by the adoption of a common framework. This is certainly the case with the segmentation of the Latin verbal or nominal forms. It may however well be that the differences are largely dispelled once a common framework is adopted for the language in question. Two descriptions of a Semitic language would differ entirely according to whether discontinuous (broken) segments are allowed or not. But if agreement is reached here, a fair degree of matchability should be possible. The traditional typology sets the Semitic languages fairly and squarely among the inflexional languages, on a par with Latin or Greek. The resemblance was expressed by saying that in all these languages stems and inflexions constituted together a closely knit, indeed indivisible, unit, as opposed to the agglutinative languages, where they were, so to speak, loosely strung together. But the resemblance is rather superficial, since once discontinuous segments are permitted in the description of a Semitic language, a determinate segmentation is often attainable. For the early Indo-European languages, on the other hand, no such device is adequate to restore determinacy. Division is more often feasible in Latin than in Arabic if broken segments are disallowed in both, and is less often feasible if broken segments are allowed in both; but in either case the segmentation will be more determinate for Arabic than for Latin.

Similarly the common comparison of the class-indeterminacy of English with that of Chinese cannot be pursued very far; many of the indeterminacies of English may be removed by the adoption of a given framework, yielding large and relatively well-defined classes of minimal segments.

One solution to the problem of segmentation is to operate with rules for transforming one larger segment into another, rather than with analyses of this larger segment into smaller segments.[1] In the same way, rules of class-transformation may be an alternative to allotting units to one or another of some sub-class, independently of their functional role in the sentence. Normally, such terms as 'subject' and 'object' differ from such terms as 'noun' and 'pronoun' by having their place in a scheme of class-transformations rather than of classes. Obviously, however, the two sets of terms could be treated analogously: thus 'noun' and 'verb' in English could be given a class-transformational role.

It will be seen that although up to a point our provisional typology appears to be in agreement with the tradition, identity even along this one dimension cannot be assumed. In any case, since the traditional typology was not explicitly

[1] Cf. C. F. Hockett, 'Two Models of Grammatical Description', *Word*, 10.

based on any general principle, the number of dimensions involved could not be known.

The traditional typology allowed for a fourth type, the 'polysynthetic'. This type deserved the self-contradictory definition of the Oxford Dictionary: 'characterized by combining several words of a sentence into one word.' The term is hardly used any longer even by linguists who, in private conversation at least, readily avail themselves of the other traditional terms.

All the problems confronting the analyst may be represented as problems of asymmetry, of non-correspondence. Linguists seek to assimilate one level to another, and do this in different ways, by the exclusion from their systems of one or the other asymmetry.

This is true even of those linguists who make it a declared principle to treat each level in turn, seeking the correspondence between them afterwards, as is characteristic of the so-called Yale School. In effect they set up barriers between certain levels, but apply the principle of maximal symmetry to those which lie in between. For instance, a phonological level is distinguished, governed by the main criteria of intrinsic phonetic similarity and complementary distribution, together with the important subsidiary criterion of pattern-congruity. Pattern-congruity means the maximal correspondence between intrinsic phonetic qualities and distribution. It is really quite arbitrary that intrinsic qualities and distribution should not be regarded as different levels. True, they are difficult, or better impossible to separate entirely in the process of constructing a system, but then just the same holds of any different levels.

Or to take a morphological problem in the form in which it has arisen in the Yale School. Traditional grammar has it that there are four morphological segments in Latin *cīvis bonus*. Current American analysis, so far as the four segments are concerned, conforms to the tradition. But one American linguist

(Professor Zellig Harris) treats *-is -us* as one single discontinuous or 'broken' segment.[1] Why? Roughly, because the total segment *cīvis bonus* does not permit the replacement of *-is* by another segment independently of the replacement of *-us* by another segment. He seeks to restore the symmetry between segments and freely contrasting units: reasonably enough, since contrast in *some* environments is the main criterion for morphological segmentation. He is prepared to do this at the cost of continuity, another criterion of unit-segments.

Now it should be easy to see that any definition of congruence based on the traditional analysis would be quite inapplicable here. The traditional definition of congruence relied on the recurrence, in a syntagm, of segments referable to the same morpheme. But on Harris's interpretation there is no recurrence. It would be of small importance if his interpretation threw out only instances of 'congruence' over which there might be hesitation. But it is the model examples which are affected.

However, the fundamental asymmetry offered by the Latin material is bound to be revealed in some form or another. In Harris's system it would reappear as 'morph-discontinuity over open juncture'. There remains, therefore, the possibility of a *pre-grammatical* statement which is neutral with regard to the different grammatical statements and indeed basic to both of them.

We have not yet learnt to speak well in the problem-language—to stand back, so to speak, from the grammatical descriptions, and to state in more primitive terms the problems which give rise to the differences between them. Hence we constantly find ourselves using the language of linguistic analysis when we should be using a 'pre-grammatical' language.

However, there is already the beginning of a pre-grammatical vocabulary. Linguists speak of their rough material in terms

[1] Z. Harris, *Methods in Structural Linguistics*, Chicago, 1951.

48

of 'prospective phonemes' and 'prospective morphemes'—the object of the word *prospective* being to take the words *phoneme* and *morpheme* out of their natural context in linguistic description. The word *indeterminacy* itself clearly does not belong to the language of analysis, while even *class* and *segment* are relatively recent introductions. Perhaps they could better be confined to the pre-grammatical terminology, other terms, such as *form* and *category*, being restricted to use in the final descriptions.

Now I wish to consider an objection that I have so far met only in passing. It is that linguists, however much they may disagree over the application of such grammatical terms as *word*, at least agree on the model examples. One of them extends the term in one direction, another in another. But so long as they agree on the model examples, a typology on this basis is possible. The other examples will fit in as borderline cases.

Clearly, borderline problems will arise, and they can be accommodated as such. But with the grammatical terms it is not just an affair of borderline cases. Grammatical terms overlap in such a way that what is central in the category of one linguist may be at the margin of the category of another. Of course, this is not *always* so, and our typology seeks to profit precisely by this fact. To say, as we have, that for this or that language linguists may match their segments or their classes, is to say that, for *these* languages, at least the nuclear cases of segment or class, respectively, may be matched. The differences here, of kind and degree, may be made the basis of a general typology.

The Study of the Mother-Tongue

An inaugural lecture delivered on 21 February 1961 by
RANDOLPH QUIRK, *Professor of English Language in
the University of London (University College)*

The Study of the Mother-Tongue

It is common practice in Inaugural Lectures to make to one's predecessors in the Chair some due and proper reference: gracefully, interestingly, piously—and often, indeed, sincerely. It has been my fortune, however, to be honoured with election to two Chairs of which I was to be the first incumbent, and so I have been denied the use of this convenient and appropriate theme. There is, nevertheless, some comfort in even this degree of common ground between the present occasion and my inauguration in Durham. It is not always so, and an earlier Professor of English in this College had a radically different experience. A few years after delivering his inaugural lecture on English studies here, R. G. Latham was reading his inaugural lecture on medicine at the Middlesex Hospital, and the two lectures are printed as the first items in his *Opuscula*, their juxtaposition silently invoking the reader's astonishment. On Professor Latham I wish to say more presently, but the mention of his name at this point fittingly reminds us that, so far from my new Chair representing the beginning of a new study here, teaching and research in the English language have had a long and spectacular history from the early days of the College's foundation to the present time and the distinguished work of Professor A. H. Smith.[1]

The situation which has called this new Chair into existence is the awareness—newly acute, but which has been increasing with redoubled momentum since the war—of the central importance of English language studies, not merely in this College and University, not merely in this country, but in the

[1] In connexion with the present lecture, I am indebted to Professor A. H. Smith, Mr J. Scott, Miss A. P. Duckworth, Mr J. P. L. Rusiecki, Dr A. H. King, and Mr C. Blagden for much welcome help in the course of discussion and correspondence; to the BBC for giving access to talks material; and to Mr Hilary Corke for permission to quote from his work.

world. We have become better informed about the function of language in society. We have become more concerned about the place of language in education and about the need for a linguistic discipline, since it is through language that man looks at his world and in fact by means of language that he segments his world. The decline of Latin in our education system has not therefore reduced the need for a linguistic discipline: it has merely added to the responsibilities of the English teacher, as the linguistic discipline comes more and more to have English both as its vehicle and as its object. Moreover, the vastly expanded educational programme of our time means that we must train a far higher proportion of our population than hitherto to make sophisticated use of English in their communication with each other in the higher levels of study, in the arts and sciences alike.

Similarly, the emergence of the underdeveloped countries, both within and without the Commonwealth, has meant not a decrease in the use and teaching of English, but a phenomenal increase, as these countries seek to maintain or establish contact with more advanced areas through the use of the world's chief international language. The situation which C. K. Ogden clearly foresaw between the wars, and for which he ingeniously sought to provide with his British, American, Scientific, International, and Commercial form of English, has now fully developed. It was with the manifold problems of this situation in view that the Communication Research Centre was formed here in 1953, and its attention has been focused on them.

In December 1960, at a Conference of Professors of English, Education, and Linguistics, it was clearly recognized that all the problems just mentioned—even the most formidable and seemingly most remote—are in the last analysis intimately linked with the urgent need to augment and improve the teaching of English language at all levels in Great Britain. For we must realize that, whether we like it or not, we in this country have special and inescapable responsibilities for the maintenance and propagation of English, responsibilities which devolve upon us by virtue of our history, the Commonwealth, our partnership in the English-speaking world, and—not least—our prestige as the cradle of English. The title of Professor MacKenzie's recent inaugural lecture, *The Outlook for English in Central Africa*,[1] is symptomatic of present concerns and implies a challenge which we must not fail to accept.

2

The position of English today may perhaps assume greater clarity if it is seen in perspective, against the background of Shakespeare's time and the new assertion of the English language. In Richard Mulcaster's England, English was still in competition with Latin on account of the wealth of learning registered in it and because of its value for conferring with other nations. 'Which two considerations being fullie answered,' says Mulcaster in 1582,[2] namely 'that we seke [the learned tongues] from *profit* & kepe them for that conference, whatsoeuer else maie be don in our tung, either to serue priuat vses, or the beawtifying of our speche, I do not se, but it maie well be admitted, euen tho in the end it displaced the *Latin*.' As well as having this to say on his age's version of the 'compulsory Latin' question, he interestingly draws attention to the possibility that English may enlarge its scope.

Will all kindes of trade, and all sorts of traffik, make a tung of account? If the spreading sea, and the spacious land could vse anie speche, theie would both shew you, where, and in how manie strange places, theie haue sene our peple, and also giue you to wit, that theie deall in as much, and as great varietie of matters, as anie other peple do, whether at home or abrode. . . . Now all this varietie of matter, and diuersitie of trade, make both matter for speche, & mean to enlarge it.

[1] Oxford University Press, 1960.
[2] *The First Part of the Elementarie*; quotations are from Ch. 13 and the Peroration.

Moreover, even if one kept strictly to the facts of the present, even though 'our English tung', as he says, 'is of small reatch, it stretcheth no further then this Ilād of ours, naie not there ouer all'; even though 'our state is no *Empire* to hope to enlarge it by commāding ouer cuntries'; even though the language en-shrines 'no rare cunning . . . to cause forenners studie it': nevertheless, it is worth fostering because it is our native tongue.

Within the century that followed, the situation changed radically. English did not remain 'of small reatch', trade and exploration enlarged it in all senses, and there came to be no dearth of foreigners eager to study it. One hundred and fifty years after Mulcaster's death, we find Thomas Sheridan, the dramatist's father, fully alive to what is essentially the modern position and urging that major steps be taken to meet it. His words have an even greater irony for us than Mulcaster's, for we have been slow to take up his suggestions. In his *Lectures on Elocution*, published in 1762, he sees as a 'prerequisite for the improvement of education' and in consequence 'the benefit of these realms', a thorough 'grammatical knowledge of our mother tongue, and a critical skill therein'. These desired ends will be best achieved, he says, by 'the establishment of these studies at the two Universities; as in those will be found collected all such as are hereafter to be masters of schools, who by learning the English grammar themselves . . . will of course be enabled to teach' it 'throughout the kingdom' (pp. 195–7). Along with these lectures, Sheridan published in 1762 a *Dissertation On the Causes of the Difficulties which occur in learning the English Tongue*, so concerned is he for the foreigners who are seeking to learn English and by the almost total lack of facilities offered them in this country. In the Dedication of this *Dissertation*, he makes a powerful appeal for help to establish an institution 'for the study of the English language'.

To these quotations from Mulcaster and Sheridan, I should like to add one more to complete these notes on the emergence

56

of our present-day situation. It is from the Minute which Macaulay wrote on 2 February 1835, when a decision had to be taken on whether to pursue education in the Sub-Continent through the medium of one of the major oriental languages or whether to turn to English for this purpose:

We have to educate a people who cannot at present be educated by means of their mother-tongue. We must teach them some foreign language. The claims of our own language it is hardly necessary to recapitulate. It stands pre-eminent even among the languages of the West. It abounds with works of imagination not inferior to the noblest which Greece has bequeathed to us; with models of every species of eloquence; with historical compositions . . .; with just and lively representations of human life and human nature; with the most profound speculations on metaphysics, morals, government, jurisprudence, and trade; with full and correct information respecting every experimental science. . . . Whoever knows that language has ready access to all the vast intellectual wealth which all the wisest nations of the earth have created and hoarded in the course of ninety generations . . . [English] is likely to become the language of commerce throughout the seas of the East. It is the language of two great European communities which are rising, the one in the south of Africa, the other in Australasia. . . . Whether we look at the intrinsic value of our literature or at the particular situation of [India], we shall see the strongest reason to think that, of all foreign tongues, the English tongue is that which would be the most useful to our native subjects.[1]

As Macaulay's nephew, Sir George Trevelyan, has said,[2] this Minute 'set the question at rest at once and for all', and just as history has endorsed the necessarily limited vision of Mulcaster, so it has the understandably wider one of Macaulay.

3

When Macaulay wrote his Minute, there had been a Chair of English for some years in an English university which was not itself in existence when Sheridan pleaded for the establishment of such studies in Oxford and Cambridge. And four years after

[1] G. M. Young, *Macaulay: Prose and Poetry* (London, 1952), pp. 722–3.
[2] *The Life and Letters of Lord Macaulay* (London, 1908), p. 292.

Macaulay's Minute, this Chair came to be occupied by that too little remembered scholar, Robert Gordon Latham.

I do not mean that Latham has been forgotten within University College. Professor Smith paid tribute to him in his inaugural lecture eleven years ago, and at the time of the College's centenary his memory was kept alive by Sir Israel Gollancz, Professor R. W. Chambers, and Professor Hale Bellot. But little attempt has been made to assess his place more widely in the history of philology and English language studies. While Holger Pedersen[1] refers very briefly to his attack on the theory of the Asian origin of Indo-European, most historians of our subject make no mention of him at all. It need cause little surprise, therefore, that he is completely ignored in one of the largest and most recent treatments, that of Hans Arens, whose voluminous *Sprachwissenschaft* of 1955 gives due credit to J. V. Stalin and some four hundred others for their services to language study, but who in fact pays scant attention to any British linguist later than Horne Tooke. Yet, for a quarter of a century after his appointment here, Latham was in the very forefront of British linguistics, with a considerable international reputation. He was, as Theodore Watts said, 'one of the first men inquired after by the celebrity-hunting foreigner in London'.[2] I have thought it fitting, therefore, to single out this one man from among earlier Professors of English here, as deserving our better remembrance in the years ahead.

Latham was born in Lincolnshire, where his father was the Vicar of Billingborough. Like Richard Mulcaster, his great predecessor in the study of English, he went to Eton (of which he became captain) and King's College, Cambridge. Indeed, he is reported as saying that his father marked him from birth for a Fellowship at King's, and this parental ambition was realized in 1832, when he was just twenty, and he held it until

---

[1] *Sprogvidenskaben i det nittende Aarhundrede* (Copenhagen, 1924), p. 293.
[2] *Athenæum* (17 March 1888).

1848. Amidst his other early literary activities, he displays his concern for English in a publication which appeared in 1834, entitled *An Address to the Authors of England and America on the Necessity and Practicability of Permanently Remodelling their Alphabet and Orthography*. It begins[1] with somewhat unendearing words which remind us of how uncompromising a man may be at twenty-two: 'The obscurest individual among you . . . works . . . towards the production of what may be called the literature of the age we live in.' Perhaps because so few of his readers were prepared to identify themselves with this 'obscurest individual', Latham's spelling-reform tract appears to have made little impact.[2] Soon after its appearance, he went abroad and studied philology in Germany and Scandinavia, and in Norway he made the acquaintance of a young Manxman, Edward Forbes, three years his junior and the future Professor of Botany at King's College, London. It was perhaps his travels at this time which gave Latham the pseudonym 'Travelling Bachelor' in the 1840's, when he was prominent in a gay circle which included Edward Forbes and Latham's brother-in-law, Edward Creasy, then Professor of History at University College and later knighted. The circle was the Tipperary Hall set, who used to carouse at the Wellington in Highgate, and whose jocular ballads and conversational links were published in *Bentley's Miscellany*. But that is another story.

In 1839 Latham accepted the appointment here as Professor of English, and although he did not retain the Chair for many years, his tenure was of the utmost importance for English and linguistic studies both within the College and (especially by reason of the Philological Society) more widely in the country as a whole. Moreover, it was his teaching experience here that fitted him to make the enormous contribution in grammar-

---

[1] According to the abridged copy in the British Museum.
[2] But his *Defence of Phonetic Spelling* of 1872 showed that this was a subject that continued to interest him.

writing through which his name became a household word for much of Queen Victoria's reign. While still at University College he pursued medicine along with his other studies and duties, and in 1842 he became a Licentiate (and in 1846 a Fellow) of the Royal College of Physicians. He proceeded to the degree of M.D. in 1844 and in the same year was appointed Assistant Physician at the Middlesex Hospital, having already been serving there as lecturer in forensic medicine and materia medica. He resigned his Chair here a year later. In 1849 he left the Middlesex Hospital to develop his interest in ethnology, yet a further sphere in which he was to make a notable contribution, and in 1852 he took up duties for a time as Director of the Ethnological Department at the Crystal Palace.

To outline thus sketchily Latham's biography only up to the age of forty, by which time he had achieved both learning and high office in three quite distinct areas of professional life, is enough to show the extraordinary stature of the man: enough to make it seem perfectly natural that by this time, too, he had for some years enjoyed the honour of being a Fellow of the Royal Society. One further scrap of information may help to sharpen the image of his distinction. To show how fortunate Watts-Dunton had been in the company he kept, eight names only are given in the list of great friendships which he enjoyed; the eight are Swinburne, the Rossettis, William Morris, Matthew Arnold, Tennyson, Borrow, Lowell, and Latham.[1]

4

But of course it is not his life but his scholarly writings to which I wish to draw attention. To be more precise, since he was prolific and wrote in several fields, I shall restrict discussion to a small selection of his writings. He has to his credit about thirty

[1] T. Watts-Dunton, *Old Familiar Faces* (London, 1916); all of the circle have attracted biographers, except Latham.

books alone, and even this is to exclude texts that he merely edited. In addition, between 1844 and 1860 he published more than two dozen papers in the *Reports* of the British Association for the Advancement of Science, of which he remained a member till 1874. During roughly the same period—from 1842 to 1858—he delivered a further and more distinguished two dozen papers to the Philological Society, in the history of which he figured far more prominently than is now generally realized. This was, until Latham's time at University College, a student association, albeit with a rather middle-aged name, The Society for Philological Inquiries. Latham was one of the small band of enthusiasts who contrived to make it the nation-wide learned body that it remains today. The change that befell this undergraduate society R. W. Chambers refers to (in an expression which had topical overtones in the twenties) as the 'dictatorship of the professoriate';[1] today we might prefer to call it a 'take-over bid by the directors of the Professorial Board'. Latham was a foundation member of the reconstituted society and a member of the Council for its first eighteen years.

A good many of his articles are on ethnological subjects, and these we must obviously pass over on the present occasion, though it should be remembered that he was, as a contemporary put it, the father of a brilliant school of ethnology, and that he published half a dozen important books in this field, culminating in the two-volumed work, *Descriptive Ethnology*, in 1859. For the rest, his contributions for the British Association and the Philological Society are in various areas of philology: classical philology and prosody; comparative philology; and 'developmental' and 'general' philology—or, as we would usually call them today, historical and general linguistics. On the latter, I should like to draw attention, in passing, to his wealth of writings not only on relatively accessible languages such as those in the Celtic, Slavonic, Ottoman, or even Caucasian

[1] *Philologists at University College* (London, 1927), p. 20.

groups, but also on American Indian, African, Papuan, and other exotic languages, which established in the Philological Society a tradition of studying the living non-Indo-European languages which has so flourished in our own time, especially with the work of scholars in the School of Oriental and African Studies.

The results of Latham's phenomenally extensive learning in all these fields of philology were brought together in his 700-page volume, *Elements of Comparative Philology*, which was published in 1862 and dedicated to Prince Louis Bonaparte, nephew of Napoleon the Great and a resident in this country where he was active in linguistic research, particularly in the field of Basque studies. (Through the two millennia from Mithridates to Prince Trubetzkoy, linguistics has been, if not the sport of kings, at least a not infrequent and perfectly respectable hobby of royalty.) It was through this book that he gave widest currency to his theory that the Indo-European languages had their ancient home in Europe rather than in Asia, setting at naught the views of Bopp, Grimm, and Müller, and indeed accusing his opponents (who comprised virtually the entire philological 'establishment') of baseless assumption. His arguments were greeted with scornful incredulity, and there can be no question that his influence and prestige in the most learned circles declined sharply from that time. Theodore Watts, writing Latham's obituary in 1888,[1] says on this point that if it should be found that Latham was right and his opponents wrong, history would find it difficult to assign him too high a place in the scholarly hierarchy of the nineteenth century. Today, most scholars would agree that Latham's opponents were indeed wrong, though history has done little about it and Latham seldom emerges from oblivion except in occasional inaugural addresses.

[1] *Athenæum* (17 March 1888).

5

I may well, by this time, have given the impression to those unacquainted with Latham's work that he devoted his energies to almost any study in preference to English, the subject in which he held his Chair at University College. If so, I must hasten to make amends. Latham was deeply interested in both our language and our literature throughout his life, and one might just mention that it is among his very last works that we find the *Two Dissertations on Hamlet*. In his inaugural lecture, delivered on 14 October 1839, he dutifully divided his attention and time between the linguistic and literary programmes on which he discoursed. What he had to say about the study of language on that occasion is not only of the utmost importance for an assessment of Latham: it is also highly relevant to our own times and for the further development of our work.

In the first place, we must note his insistence that it is contemporary languages that we must study in order to observe philological processes. Such an approach cannot fail, I think, to remind us of that greater linguist, Henry Sweet, who was born in the year of Latham's resignation from the Chair here and whose magnificent contribution to linguistics has been fully and fittingly extolled by Professor Wrenn[1] and the late Professor Firth. Let me read you some words uttered by Sweet in 1877, which Firth loved (as he himself put it) 'to quote in every suitable context'[2]: 'Our tendency is not so much towards the antiquarian philology, and text-criticism in which German scholars have done so much, as towards the observation of the phenomena of living languages. . . . Our aim ought clearly to be, while assimilating the methods and results of German work, to

[1] *Transactions of the Philological Society 1946*, pp. 177–201.
[2] *Trans. Phil. Soc. 1951*, p. 72; see also *Trans. Phil. Soc. 1946*, p. 131, and *Archivum Linguisticum*, 1 (1949), p. 109. Sweet's words are quoted from *Trans. Phil. Soc. 1877–9*, p. 13.

concentrate our energies mainly on what may be called "living philology".'

Beside Sweet's important and forward-looking words, whose place in linguistic history has long been assured, I should like to set these of Latham, spoken in University College nearly forty years earlier:

We draw too much upon the Philologists of Germany . . . I believe that the foundations of etymology are to be laid upon the study of existing processes; and I grow sanguine when I remember that by no one as well as by an Englishman can these processes be collected . . . The details of Etymology I can willingly give up to the scholars of the Continent . . .: but for the *Principles* of Etymology, I own to the hope that it may be the English School that shall be the first to be referred to and the last to be distrusted.[1]

(By 'etymology', one should add, Latham means what we broadly call 'grammar' and he sometimes calls it 'grammatical etymology'; for what we call 'etymology' today, dealing with the individual histories of words, he uses the term 'historical etymology'.) It is noteworthy that the features which make Sweet's words outstanding are here strikingly anticipated by Latham: that, in the era when most energies were devoted to the historical field and when the most exciting philological advances were being made therein, the need should be so clearly felt to strike out in the direction of 'living philology', the observation of 'existing processes'; that an English School should have the temerity to challenge German scholarship; and that this School should specifically seek the principles and systems underlying the mass of details.

There is one further argument which Latham advanced in his inaugural lecture which is also of particular relevance for us today. He claims the 'Sufficiency of the English Language as a Disciplinal Study . . . irrespective of the fact of its being the native language of Englishmen'. If we detect here a defensive note arising from the theory of the claim, it has completely

[1] *An Inaugural Lecture* (London, 1840), pp. 9, 16–18.

64

gone when Latham returns to this point a year or so later. In *The English Language*, published in 1841, it is not merely that the native language is a *sufficient* study; it is now claimed to be the best. In the first place, he insists that the study of the mother-tongue (and my title today is an echo of his theme) is basic in education: 'With the results of modern criticism, as applied to his native tongue, it is conceived that an educated Englishman should be familiar' (p. v). Secondly, his views have become firmer as to why linguistic studies are best accomplished through the native tongue: 'If it be true that the Theory of a Language is best understood after the Practice of it has been acquired, the fittest disciplinal study in general Grammar, for the native of any country whatever, is the structure of his own Mother-tongue' (p. vii). Again, the Preface to his *English Grammar* of 1843: 'Whatever be the country of the student, the analysis of his native tongue is his best practice in general grammar' (p. vi).

A few years later, in a lecture to the Royal Institution in 1854, he broadens his argument, further endorsing Sheridan's plea which I quoted earlier, and providing us with further reason to renew acquaintance with Latham as these matters assume a new topicality in the context of such present-day talking points as English Language at 'A' Level, and the extension of linguistics in the universities. The lecture was entitled, 'On the Importance of the Study of Language as a Branch of Education for All Classes', and Latham told his audience that 'the study of Speech would find place in a well-devised system of education, even if the tongues of the whole wide world were reduced to a single language, and that language to a single dialect'. Such a view has found increasing favour in recent years: that language study is not merely of relevance in learning a foreign language or the history of one's own language, but in studying any aspect of human behaviour, since language is the most important single characteristic of human behaviour. In

65

the words of Professor James Sledd, which I have quoted on other occasions: 'Man is the speaking animal. That is the main reason for studying speech'.[1] To Latham, too, the value of grammar lies in the scientific study of an instrument, a communication medium; therefore, he says, 'the language which the grammar so studied should represent, must be the mother-tongue of the student. . . . This study is the study of a theory', and since the study of a theory can be most conveniently pursued if preliminary drills can be dispensed with, it follows that 'a man's mother-tongue is the best medium for the elements of scientific philology'. There is much truth in this and although it would seem that frequent reference to one's knowledge of at least one foreign language is necessary to gain *the fullest insight* into the structure of one's own, it is surely true nevertheless that the fullest insight into linguistic processes is to be achieved in relation to one's native language, since it is given to few of us to attain comparable *Sprachgefühl* in any other. To this extent Latham is right, and his words emphasize the special responsibility carried by those whose task is to teach the mother-tongue.

6

We see, then, that even after leaving University College, where he established English language studies on principles which we do well to bear in mind today, he continued to develop his fertile ideas on the place of language studies in education, just as he continued, by his rich contributions, to develop the Philological Society's interests in the directions in which Sweet was later to move with such brilliance and vigour. He came to stress increasingly the geographical spread of English, as for instance in his *Elements of English Grammar for the Use of Ladies' Schools*, which appeared in 1849. Even this little book of a

[1] *Language*, XXXIV (1958), p. 139.

hundred pages, printed in Gower Street, and sold for one shilling and sixpence, begins by describing the world-wide dissemination of English and gives a brief historical account of how this came about. This aspect is further developed in his book, *The English Language*, which in 1862 appeared in a fifth edition, having grown from a work of just over four hundred pages in 1841 to what is virtually an entirely new book almost twice as extensive. In addition to the relation between British and American English (to this day all too often ignored in our studies), he discusses the English of South Australia—then a recent development—and even such deviant forms of our language as thieves' slang and Taki-taki, a creolized form of English with an admixture of Dutch, spoken in Surinam. The historical statements, moreover, have come to be usefully supported not merely by early forms but by quotations from early grammarians—particularly Wallis, for whom Latham had a high regard. His early insistence on observation of current phenomena has borne fruit in his own increased sophistication in matters such as usage. By 1862, he has grown cool on the value of appeal to the written language, to history, or to scholars; instead, he sees usage as determined by imitation, so that one finds one's index rather in 'educated bodies, such as the bar, the pulpit, the senate', because of the 'quantities of imitators that, irrespective of the worth of his pronunciation, each individual can carry with him. On this latter ground', he adds, perhaps with resignation, 'the stage is a sort of standard' (p. 448).

He takes the discussion of usage further in his *Comparative Philology*, again anticipating Sweet in trying to educate public opinion in the direction of an objective approach to language. If language, he says, 'at all times and in all places, stands in the same relation to its ideas as an exponent, it is equally good as language', a view which continues to be misunderstood, though it has been reiterated by Sweet, Bloomfield, and others, from Latham's day to this. While he himself feels that the expression 'bad grammar' is most reasonably to be applied to grammatical statements by a grammarian who has done his work badly, Latham fully sees that such labels are conveniently and inevitably applied with entirely different reference by the speaker of a language from the vantage point of his speech community. But we must understand how parochial, relative, and impermanent that vantage point is. What is called 'bad grammar', says Latham, is a detail in which a speaker differs from someone else who calls *his* form of speech 'good grammar', but imperfect and misguided writings on this subject have confused the issue and obscured the quite separate 'philological truth that *whatever is, is right*'. The man who says *I are* instead of *I am* is reacting to 'unconscious analogies'. While it is true that in England such a speaker would be correctly regarded as belonging to an illiterate stratum of society, yet if such speakers 'formed a community by themselves in (say) an island of the Pacific, and were visited by a missionary there, who formed his grammar solely on what he found . . . the vulgarism would become classical. . . . No one calls *jeg er* bad Danish.' It follows that in itself a development like *I are* 'is as little to be condemned as the conservative force which would have resisted it is to be praised'.[1]

Just as his thinking in general linguistics continued to mature till his later years when we have a small distillation of his accumulated learning in the *Outlines of General or Developmental Philology* (1878), so too on specifically English grammar we find some of his best and most thoughtful work in the slender volume, *Essential Rules and Principles for the Study of English Grammar*, of 1876. It would of course be easy to find fault with his description of English: the grammarian has yet to be born of whom this cannot be said. In all his linguistic work, he tended to be unduly influenced by logic (as witness,

[1] *Elements of Comparative Philology* (London, 1862), esp. p. 702.

in particular, his *Logic and its Application to Language* of 1856), and this frequently mars his handling of English grammar. Moreover, as a product of his age, he is inevitably capable of basing prescriptive statements, particularly in his earlier work, upon largely irrelevant (and sometimes incorrect) historical data. But as early as 1843, he comes near to an 'immediate constituent' analysis of nominal groups like the *king of Saxony's army*, he defines *case* on formal lines which remain acceptable, and for his time makes excellent statements on the function of accent in English.[1] In *A Handbook of the English Language*, which first appeared in 1851, we find such deductions as 'The convertibility of words is in the inverse ratio to the amount of their inflection', and by *inflection* here he means 'peculiar signs expressive of . . . particular parts of speech'; thus a verb *count* can come to be used as a noun more readily than one like *rarify* which has a verb-forming affix. It is of interest to note his disapproval of the terms 'strong' and 'weak', as applied to conjugational distinctions: Sweet so shared his distaste as to replace them by the more descriptive labels 'vocalic' and 'consonantal'. On a point that is more than terminological, Latham observed that 'Notwithstanding its name, the present tense, in English, does not express a strictly *present* action',[2] and the modern reader recalls the rediscovery of this fact by descriptive linguists which has led some American structuralists to speak of the English tenses as 'past' and 'non-past'.[3]

A later work than the *Handbook* containing interesting observations on English grammar is a fifty-page section of the Preface to the revised edition of *Johnson's Dictionary* which Latham completed in 1866 for Longmans, with which firm he had very

[1] *An Elementary English Grammar* (London, 1843), §§ 296, 307, 312.

[2] *A Handbook of the English Language*, 2nd ed. (London, 1855), §§ 266, 284, 320; this book had run to an eighth edition by 1878.

[3] For example, G. L. Trager and H. L. Smith, Jr., in *An Outline of English Structure* (Norman, Okla., 1951), p. 77.

close relations from about 1860 onwards.[1] He is increasingly concerned to find formal criteria in preference to semantic ones. It is here that we are told that parts of speech can best be distinguished according as words are able to occupy various positions in constructions. It is here, too, that he dwells most thoughtfully on such criteria as accent and frequency of collocation not only to distinguish compound words from word-groups but also to describe the differing degrees of cohesion between words, as in expressions like *make bold*. Again like Sweet after him, he draws attention to an area of linguistic description which falls between the ordinarily conceived provinces of the lexicographer and the grammarian, and he regrets (as we do still) that so little work has been done on it.[2]

7

The modernity of Latham's thinking, and the recognition that he was tackling educational and linguistic problems which are still with us, naturally lead us to take a brief look at the present. In many ways our situation has grown more complicated: our present educational system and policy make the extension of English language teaching more urgent than a century ago. In particular, the demand for English teaching overseas has grown immeasurably, and even in those countries with a long and excellent record for teaching English, there is much to be done. The Rev. B. T. Croft[3] has told us within the last few months of a religious fraternity in Switzerland which appealed for funds from English-speaking travellers by displaying a sign which

[1] See R. Quirk and J. Warburg, 'James Eyre: Annotator', *English Studies*, xxxix (1958), esp. p. 244. Mr. C. Blagden has kindly supplied information on Latham's connexion with Longmans, and it is also referred to in T. G. Hake, *Memoirs of Eighty Years* (London, 1892), where there are interesting notes on Latham, pp. 205 ff.
[2] See my paper, 'Towards a Description of English Usage', *Trans. Phil. Soc. 1960*, pp. 42, 56f.
[3] *The English-Speaking World* (September 1960), p. 32.

read: 'The Brothers harbour every kind of disease and have no regard whatever for religion.'

There are of course many good grammars for teaching English to foreigners, but we cannot achieve first-rate ones until we have first-rate grammars for our own use in the English-speaking countries. And these in turn cannot be produced to our proper satisfaction until there has been a major operation in the observation of 'existing processes' in our language, just as Latham recommended in 1839. In the same way, our trustworthy desk-dictionaries today could not have evolved without the immense root-and-branch inquiry into our lexical resources which produced the vast *New English Dictionary*. The Survey of Educated English Usage, which began in Durham and which is now being conducted at University College with generous support from Messrs. Longmans, Green and the Clarendon Press, seeks to carry out this large-scale observation, and we are fortunate in having the active co-operation of the Talks Division of the BBC (who are understandably concerned to extend knowledge of natural speech behaviour), and of scholars in Edinburgh, Leeds, and other universities, both in this country and abroad.

The principles on which the Survey is being conducted I have described elsewhere,[1] and it is unnecessary on this occasion to dwell on these. Of the needs which primarily called the Survey into being—the deficiencies at all educational levels in the English-speaking countries—fresh evidence is ever accumulating. On 7 February 1961, *The Times* printed an article on these deficiencies as they related to the United States, deploring the fact that 'More than 94 per cent. of the colleges at which elementary school-teachers are training have no systematized study of the history and structure of the English language. More than 61 per cent. do not require a course in English grammar and its use.'

[1] *Trans. Phil. Soc. 1960*, pp. 40–61.

Let it not be supposed that we in this country are in an appreciably stronger position, or that educated opinion here is well-informed about the 'existing processes' of English. For the majority of us, what we know about English is what has been handed down by grammatological tradition, and little enough of that was ever based on observation. One small example must suffice. Bishop Lowth is typical among the influential early grammarians who insisted that no pause could come between the elements of a simple sentence.[1] Such a pedantic approach to the cadences of spoken English was ridiculed, we remember, by Laurence Sterne:

—And how did *Garrick* speak the soliloquy last night?—Oh, against all rule, my Lord,—most ungrammatically! betwixt the substantive and the adjective, which should agree together in *number, case,* and *gender,* he made a breach thus—stopping, as if the point wanted settling;—and betwixt the nominative case, which your lordship knows should govern the verb, he suspended his voice in the epilogue a dozen times, three seconds, and three-fifths by a stop-watch, my Lord, each time . . . —But in suspending his voice—was the sense suspended likewise? . . . I look'd only at the stop-watch, my Lord.

Small wonder that this and similar instances of uninformed criticism cause Tristram Shandy, Gent., to exclaim: 'Grant me patience, just heaven!—Of all the cants which are canted in this canting world . . . the cant of criticism is the most tormenting!'[2]

One would hesitate to apply such immoderate language to criticism at the present time, but at least one able and generally perceptive critic of the spoken word has recently expressed views on pauses which are not at all dissimilar to those of the critic in *Tristram Shandy.* Attacking the speech-habits of television commentators and interviewers, Mr Hilary Corke particularly objects to 'the breaking up of sentences into wholly unnatural units', as when a writer is introduced 'whose

[1] *A Short Introduction to English Grammar* (London, 1762), p. 161.
[2] *Tristram Shandy* (London, 1761), vol. III, ch. 12.

first. Book has been translated into. Fourteen languages and he's. John Braine the author of. *Room at the Top*.'[1] Nor is it only critics who are thus influenced by the logic of arrangements of words as clustered and punctuated in the written forms of English. The Polish linguist Wiktor Jassem, phonetician and author of one of our best analyses of English intonation, uses such terms as 'anomalous pause' and 'misfit of a rhythmical character' of breaks like those that Mr Corke criticizes as 'unnatural'. One of Dr Jassem's examples is 'apart from. snakes'.[2]

8

Now, it would certainly appear that when someone reads aloud from the printed page, he pauses at the punctuation points rather than at these so-called 'unnatural' places. But, of course, written English read aloud is not the most typical kind of spoken English. In the impromptu speech being examined in the Survey, pauses between subject and verb, verb and object, preposition and noun are—under certain conditions—too common with all types of speakers to be designated 'unnatural' or 'anomalous', and so far as these pauses show a characteristic distribution, this distribution must appear in our description. It may well be that Mr Corke's interviewers, in trying to act a natural conversational style, overplay a single feature which they have noticed. This is a rather common state of affairs when so little objective description exists of our stylistic strata, and one must expect fictional dialogue to be in some respects more 'colloquial' than actual speech, or the village councillor to be more parliamentary than a front-bench M.P.

So little, in fact, is generally known about the caesuras of speech, after generations of orientation towards written English,

---

1 *The Listener* (26 November 1959).
2 *Intonation of Conversational English* (Wrocław, 1952), pp. 40, 91, 98.

that Mr Allen Ginsberg and other Beat poets are able to form the impression that they are almost alone in observing them. In a discussion with Mr Carne-Ross in the 'Art—Anti-Art' series on the radio a year ago, Mr Ginsberg made the extraordinary claim that the breaks and halts and so-called 'syntactic dissociations' in the Beatitude poetry represent not merely a change from the poetical tradition but an actually new speech, American speech, first properly heard and exploited in poetry by William Carlos Williams early this century. I need not now stop to illustrate these linguistic features in the work of Ginsberg and other poetniks: indeed, even in these post-Chatterley days, it is not very easy to select continuous passages from such verse that could be passed as suitable for adult audiences. I call Ginsberg's statement extraordinary, not because his poetry does not evince these phenomena, but because he thinks they are a recent development, American, and newly exploited in verse.

In his *Lectures on the Art of Reading*, of 1775, Thomas Sheridan —whom I quoted earlier—gave a warning that the enjoyment of verse was marred by an adherence to the sentential punctuation of the written form. If one failed to pause at the end of a run-on line, one failed to mark the correlation effect between the end of that line and the end of its neighbour, a correlation which, he said, was not for the eye only (II. 102 ff.). But this means admitting, in some of our best poetry, pauses of the kind that have been called 'unnatural' and 'anomalous', only recently admitted to verse, and even American. In Keats's *Lamia*, for instance,

> For the first time, since first he harboured in
> That purple-lined palace of sweet sin

or Blake's *Evening Star*

> The fleeces of our flocks are covered with
> Thy sacred dew: protect them with thine influence

we have breaks between prepositions and nominal groups, rather as in the criticized examples which I have quoted: 'the author of. *Room at the Top*' and 'apart from. snakes'. This is one of the positions in which a break has been most insistently held to be inadmissible,[1] even by those elocutionists of the late eighteenth century who deplored the restriction of pauses to positions admitting a punctuation mark; Walker states specifically that 'the *preposition* and the *noun* it governs' are 'too intimately connected to admit a pause'.[2] Such a view would naturally be upheld by the traditional equation of the English prepositional phrase with the Latin noun in oblique cases. As we have seen, however, this runs counter to the evidence in our prosody and to the evidence of the distribution of pauses in present-day speech. On the contrary, our observations are showing that, at the rank of the 'group', pauses play a role along with other features like tempo, pitch, and prominence —in indicating relative coherence within sequences of words which function as units. This may mean that, as well as appearing at points of lexical selection (as so valuably described by a colleague at University College, Dr Goldman-Eisler),[3] pauses occur in such utterances as 'apart from. snakes' and 'covered with. dew' by virtue of being at the terminals of grammatical selection.[4] In other words, a means is offered of distinguishing expressions having prepositions as proclitic to a following nominal word and expressions having prepositions as grammatically determined enclitics, these being in the category which has caused the emergence of locutions like 'he used to' and 'a house to dream of', and which interested Latham when

[1] There are, however, one or two instances acknowledged by the outstanding observer, Joshua Steele, in *An Essay Towards Establishing the Melody and Measure of Speech* (London, 1775).

[2] *Elements of Elocution* (London, 1781), p. 26.

[3] See esp. *Language and Speech*, I (1958), pp. 226–31.

[4] See the useful data in Б. Н. Аксененко, Предлоги Английского Языка (Moscow, 1956), and the statement of relationships, p. 5.

The Place of Phonetics in the University

An inaugural lecture delivered on 7 March 1961 by
N. C. SCOTT, *Professor of Phonetics in the University of London*

This lecture originally appeared as a separate publication issued in August 1961 by the School of Oriental and African Studies, University of London, in which the Chair of Phonetics is held.

The Place of Phonetics in the University

In popular use, the word 'phonetics' is understood in a number of rather vague ways relating, for the most part, to what phoneticians themselves would regard as matters of applied phonetics. Phonetics is thought of as a method of teaching pronunciation, or as in some way connected with correct pronunciation, and it is often enough necessary to explain, even in a university, that neither of these topics is a first concern of phoneticians.

To the question of teaching pronunciation I shall return later, but I make the point at once that it is the business of phonetics to study speech as it can actually be observed. Correctness of pronunciation is a matter of acceptability in particular circumstances, and the question does not arise for phoneticians until, for example, a particular kind of pronunciation has been chosen for a particular purpose. It is, of course, of immediate interest to the subject to examine the various kinds of speech that are used by groups of people with different geographical or social backgrounds, but this is not done with the object of determining what is or is not correct, except in the sense of noting the limits of actual variation within the group.

There is not uncommonly an impression that phonetic theory is complete, that its methods are established, and that all that remains is to apply them to particular languages. This impression probably goes in many cases with the tacit assumption that there are a limited number of speech sounds, most of which have been recognized, though others may remain to be discovered. I take it that this is what underlies the rather incredulous disappointment that can sometimes be observed when a phonetician is unwilling to commit himself to a statement about what, to him, is a quite inadequate amount of material.

It will be necessary, then, for me to speak of some of the problems with which we are faced in phonetics. If what I have to say about these is familiar to many of my hearers, I have the consolation of knowing that phoneticians always have the resource of listening to the lecturer instead of the lecture.

General linguists regard phonetics as a branch of their subject, and no one will deny that it is indispensable to them. Though writing is enormously important, and not even the phonetician at his purest can be unaffected by it, written language, as things have gone with human beings, depends in the long run on spoken language, and it is generally agreed that linguistics is, in the first place, concerned with living speech. It therefore follows that a general linguist must have phonetic equipment adequate to his purpose, and I do not think he could ever be said to be wastefully well equipped in this respect. But, if the linguist must have phonetic equipment, it is equally true that a phonetician must have linguistic equipment, for his interest is sounds in language, and it is thus not easy to say of any one person where the phonetician ends and the linguist begins.

It is perhaps hardly necessary to discuss the question whether phonetics is indeed a branch of general linguistics once the interdependence is admitted. I should for my part answer in the affirmative, but I hasten to say that I am happy to be a member of a department bearing the title Phonetics and Linguistics, a title that recognizes that there is a subject called phonetics, and that it is useful to speak of phoneticians as well as linguists. I also count myself fortunate in being among linguists and working in close collaboration with them.

The recognition of phonetics as a subject depends in part, as is usually the case in such matters, on practical considerations, but in any event it has a special position in relation to other linguistic studies. The title of Professor W. S. Allen's inaugural lecture in Cambridge, *On the Linguistic Study of Languages*, and the substance of the lecture itself, lays stress on a cardinal principle of contemporary linguistics, one that has not always seemed self-evident, that the analysis of a language must be made in terms of the language itself and not based on categories derived from extra-linguistic considerations.

Nevertheless, linguistics has to take account of the non-linguistic in two respects. On the one hand it is concerned with context of situation, as it was called by Professor J. R. Firth, whose recent death has meant so great a loss to both general linguistics and phonetics. In the context of situation, the language material is one element in the total of relevant features that may include persons, objects, and actions. Both the verbal and non-verbal elements are integral parts in the context of situation, and it is not simply a matter of supplying a background for the words. Verbal and non-verbal elements have thus equal status in this connexion. The internal relations of the verbal material are established at other levels of analysis, and in so far as the word 'linguistic' is strictly to be reserved for such operations, the level of context of situation is essentially non-linguistic, or at most paralinguistic. It is obviously unfortunate that the expression 'non-linguistic' should have to be used here, since the verbal elements *are* verbal, and it is because this is so that the concept is set up. There is no difficulty in making the noun 'linguistics' cover the study of context of situation, and it is very desirable that the adjective 'linguistic' should have a similar extension. What is wanted is an adjective for reference to those activities of general linguistics that are strictly concerned with the internal relations of a language, and it would perhaps be possible to use 'collinguistic' for this purpose. Context of situation would then be a linguistic, but not a collinguistic, study.

The second point of contact with the non-linguistic is precisely in the domain of phonetics. Speech depends on certain kinds of bodily activity that result in disturbances of the air, and these disturbances in their turn result, in suitable conditions, in auditory impressions. The bodily activity may be at a remove, as when we listen to a gramophone record. It may not even have involved the normal organs of speech, as when special kinds of skill are employed to produce by means of a speech-synthesizer sounds that are accepted as speech. But whatever form they take, the actions and the sound waves that directly or indirectly result from them are extra-linguistic. They are part of the outside world, and can be studied by the methods of physiology and physics. The position is similar to that for context of situation, but whereas in context of situation the linguistic and the non-linguistic items may be said to take their place side by side, at the phonetic level there is, so to speak, interpenetration, the non-linguistic serving as a vehicle for the linguistic. The study cannot therefore be left to the physiologist and physicist, since the criteria of relevance can only be determined with reference to a language. The physical nature of the material is the same for all languages; it is for the phonetician to show the significance of its features for any one language.

We enter the strictly linguistic field—or more accurately, I think, using the term I have suggested, the collinguistic field—only when we set up a system or systems for the language with which we are dealing, and it is of the utmost importance to be clear about the nature of the statements we are making: whether they are about units in a language or about what we actually hear, or think we hear. It is easy enough to fall into error in this respect, and constant vigilance is needed. At its simplest, the point may be illustrated from the use of such a term as 'voiced bilabial plosive'. This may be employed simply to call attention to the occurrence of a kind of sound that may be heard in many languages, and will convey something fairly definite to a phonetician, implying complete obstruction of the air-stream at the lips, the closure of the nasal passage by the raising of the soft palate, and activity in the larynx producing what is technically called voice. Here the term serves as the name of a class of phenomena, and nothing is said about function. If, however, voiced bilabial plosive is taken to be a unit in a system of plosives in the Sea Dayak language, the principal phonetic indication of its entering into the structure of a word will sometimes be the absence of nasal quality from a vowel following a bilabial nasal consonant. The value of a unit is determined by its place in the system.

The subject has thus an external and an internal side, and the words 'phonic' and 'phonological' have been usefully employed in connexion with the two aspects. The noun 'phonetics' should, I think, be taken to cover the study of both phonology and the phonic material. The adjective 'phonetic' is of less strict application, referring either to the whole subject or to the external side. 'Phonological' and the noun 'phonology' will then have reference to the setting up of structures and systems for particular languages, these having relations, though not necessarily simple ones, with grammatical and collocational features on the one hand and with phonic material on the other. Once these processes have been carried out, the actual sounds are, from one point of view, irrelevant; a phonological formula or unit cannot be pronounced except as the name of a phonological formula or unit.

It is less easy to be precise about the word 'phonic'. When spoken language is under discussion, the usual assumption is that we are dealing with heard sounds, and since, in what may be considered normal circumstances, both speaker and listener do hear the sounds, this works quite well for many purposes, and the term 'phonic' is appropriate for the material, which, though it cannot be called raw, has not been subjected to phonological treatment. It is not raw, for it is heard as sounds in a language, and the observer will inescapably be influenced by his past experience. I am, of course, speaking from the point of view of an investigator; to a hearer in everyday life the whole is simply given, and he reacts to it in accordance with the habits he has formed. It is to be remembered, however, that while the speaker and his hearer in some sense share the sounds that are produced, they do not hear the same thing, since the sound waves reach the speaker's ear partly by conduction through his own bones.

In any case, the bodily movements that give rise to sound form the basis of speech behaviour, and are an integral part of the total linguistic experience of every normal person. As we speak, we have sensations of touch and kinaesthetic sensations at the same time as auditory sensations, and our experience of making them, with the complex of sensations this involves, affects our recognition of sounds. We are seldom, in fact, dealing with pure sound, and the word 'phonic' must be given rather a wide extension.

The fact that our auditory impressions are private and incommunicable means that phonetics is faced with a fundamental problem in the difficulty of talking about speech sounds in such a way as to make clear what is in question. Auditory-impressionistic terms cannot be handled without some outside reference, and in fact phonetic descriptions are generally made in articulatory terms. We have a good deal of information about the kinds of articulation that occur during speech, drawn from X-ray photography and palatography as well as from direct observation and introspection, and a considerable measure of agreement is found possible about their relation to auditory impressions. The articulatory information is never exhaustive, and would be unhelpfully complex if it could be. It is, however, possible to select certain features of articulation and relate them to features of sound

84

and use them as a basis for classification. The articulatory terms are then used as names of the sound-features themselves, and in analysing speech by ear the phonetician is carrying out a kind of translation. This works well for many purposes, provided we realize what we are doing and remember that no articulation is ever simple. Our material is evanescent, extremely complex, and not neatly segmented for our purposes.

While it is sometimes comparatively easy to observe articulations, it is not always so, as in the case of vowels. Professor Daniel Jones, of whose long association with this University we are very proud, has attempted to reduce the uncertainty of reference to vowels by developing the work of Sweet and others on a scheme of cardinal vowels. He has made a gramophone record of eight vowels that may be used as points of reference for the description of others. The cardinal vowels themselves are non-linguistic in that they are not chosen as examples from any particular language or languages but simply for their convenience as a series. In deciding on his eight vowels, Jones uses articulatory criteria in two cases only. In so far as we are simply concerned to refer to a particular vowel with as little ambiguity as possible, there is no need to introduce articulatory criteria at all, but there is need to relate them to other kinds of sound by our usual process of translation, and the articulations of the remaining six are deduced from those of the two extremes. X-ray photographs indicate that the scheme is a simplification of the actual conditions for at any rate some of the intermediate vowels, but the method of description works well in practice.

It is not, of course, to be expected that there can be precise agreement on the placing of a vowel, which may in any case be made more difficult by differences of voice quality or the presence of nasality or other features. It is, however, interesting to note that Peter Ladefoged of the Phonetics Department of the University of Edinburgh has recently shown in a series of experiments that agreement is markedly closer when people have had specific training in the use of the cardinal vowels. We are at least incomparably better off than we are with descriptions such as 'the vowel of the word *cat*', or 'like the French *é*', in which both the judgement and the reference are uncertain. The sounds produced from Jones's record are at least absolute, though in this connexion I must confess to a certain regret that two recordings have been made and published. It would clearly have been difficult to forgo the advantages of electrical methods of recording, which were introduced in the interval, and no real difficulty arises, but it would have been satisfying to be able to say 'these and no others are the cardinal vowels'.

The development of electronic apparatus has made it possible to obtain a detailed record of the frequency and intensity of the sound waves produced in a stretch of speech, and it might seem that here we have the means of overcoming our difficulties of identifying and describing. It must be remembered once again, however, that speech is not made up of constant, separate sounds strung together like beads in a necklace. The records obtained would make this clear if anyone doubted it. They are in fact as complex as the sound of speech itself, and entirely neutral so far as language is concerned. The machine is, so to speak, quite unaware that it is dealing with language; it simply translates sound in visual terms. This, of course, has valuable consequences for research, but before it can be useful in the description of language material the information must be related to linguistic items, and we can at present go only a limited way with this. Much work is being done in acoustic phonetics, but much remains to be done.

Articulation is the basis of speech behaviour, and, even if our immediate material is heard sound, it could not be left out of account. As I have said, experience of making sounds plays a large part in recognizing them, and the special skills

86

a phonetician must develop and use for his work depend on his making as conscious as possible, and organizing, the experience he has of sensations of touch and kinaesthetic sensations in relation to the sounds he hears himself make. The accuracy of the observations he makes on the sounds produced by others is largely measured by his success in reproducing them. Phonetics must concern itself with all three aspects of its material, auditory, articulatory, and acoustic, and much work remains to be done on all three and their relation to one another.

Bound up with the problems of identification and description, are the problems of phonetic notation. We can do a good deal with the symbols of the International Phonetic Alphabet or similar systems, but they have limitations. Using them, we can give to someone who is familiar with the system a notion of the pronunciation of a word or phrase from a language or dialect unknown to him, but unless the transcription is accompanied by rather copious notes the notion can only be uncertain and approximate, a fact that is apt to be overlooked. Except when used for the cardinal vowels, the symbols have in general no absolute phonetic values. They can only be said to stand for certain types of sounds, and one of the difficulties is that the issue is to some extent prejudged by the provision of symbols that, in most cases, assume the dividing up of an utterance in a particular way that may not be appropriate for the language we are studying. In investigating a new language, we can, at the start, only guess at what features in the mass that is presented are relevant to our purpose, and we work by a series of experiments. In view of our increasing attention to longer stretches of speech, and to the variable persistence of particular features, there is need for a notation that will give more freedom than is allowed by the systems that are in common use. There can, of course, be no question of a notation that will give a complete record of the phonic data. It must necessarily be selective, and it is only when a phonological system is set up that the terms can be unambiguous.

It is the business of phonology to show how the phonic material serves as the vehicle for meaningful language. In saying this, I do not wish to be understood as implying that grammar and lexicon precede speech. I take them to be simply descriptive devices that help to bring order into the mass of data that confronts us when we begin to think and talk about language instead of simply using it. Phonology is another descriptive device, which provides the material in a form suitable for their use.

One line of approach is to be found in the phoneme theory, in which Daniel Jones was a pioneer, and which, in various forms, has been much used by American linguists under the name of phonemics. For the phoneme theory, the first assumption is that, in any particular language, only certain kinds of differences of sound are significant in the sense that replacement of one by another will result in a different word. On this basis, it is possible to recognize for the language a limited number of phonological units called phonemes, in terms of which any word of the language can be described. The phonemes themselves cannot be pronounced (though they can, of course, be named), but if they are symbolized and the symbols are set out in the proper order, the pronunciation of the word is unambiguously indicated to anyone who knows the rules.

The advantages of phonemic treatment for many purposes, including the reduction of unwritten languages to writing, are obvious, and of course the spirit of the method was used for orthographies long before the theory was elaborated. Its usefulness cannot be questioned, but it has shortcomings for the linguist, quite apart from what might be called its internal difficulties. The phoneme theory is essentially based on the word, and when we are dealing with longer stretches of speech difficulties arise that are not always satisfactorily resolved in terms of such concepts as assimilation and elision. It is not concerned with grammar. A phonemic transcription of the words *mates*, *maids*, and *mazes* takes no account of the fact that the diverse phonetic endings may be related to a single grammatical unit. The fact that phonemes are established for the language as a whole, irrespective of their function at particular places, tends to conceal important relations, and the fact that the method treats the material as made up of minimal segments obscures the importance of features that persist over longer stretches. As a result, it becomes necessary for certain purposes to submit the material to further processes, as, for example, morphophonemics.

An attempt to meet such difficulties is made in what is known as the prosodic approach advocated by J. R. Firth. This seeks to avoid the segmentation of phonemic analysis, abstracting features that apply to the syllable, to the word, and to still longer pieces as wholes. Prosodic analysis makes statements about the structures it sets up in terms of prosodies, referring to these features, as well as of consonants and vowels, which will thus not entirely correspond with the consonants and vowels of phonemic analysis. Instead of one system for a language as a whole, it establishes as many as are found to be appropriate for the language in question, so that it may, in particular cases, be necessary to speak of different systems for initial and final consonants, or for nominal and verbal pieces. In phonology, too, many questions await an answer.

I have mentioned the importance of distinguishing phonological statements from statements about the phonic data in general phonetic terms, but I wish to insist on the importance of not dividing the phonologist from the phonetician. Without phonetics there can be no phonology, and the better the phonetics the greater is the chance of the phonology being good.

In a well-known passage of his book *Language*, Leonard

89

Bloomfield says 'Practical phoneticians sometimes acquire great virtuosity in discriminating and reproducing all manner of strange sounds. In this, to be sure, there is some danger for linguistic work. Having learned to discriminate many kinds of sounds, the phonetician may turn to some language new or familiar and insist upon recording all the distinctions he has learned to discriminate even when in this language they are non-distinctive and have no bearing whatsoever.' Bloomfield was no enemy of phonetics, and a warning was necessary against the use of miscellaneous information about phonic data without regard to function, but the tone of the whole passage seems to me to be unfortunate in possibly suggesting that once the phonemic system is established phonetic observation has no particular linguistic interest. Even if a strictly phonemic approach is adopted, it is a phonetic observation that, in one kind of English at least, the pronunciation of the auxiliary *had* varies with the nature of its subject (if I may use that term). After a pronoun ending in a vowel, it may be said to be phonetically represented by a simple consonant, as in *he'd been there*; after a noun, even when this ends in a vowel, a weak central vowel precedes the consonant, as in *Mary had been there*; and this last pronunciation is also used when the subject is made up of a noun followed by the pronoun, as in *Mary and he had been there*. And this is of linguistic interest.

But it must be emphasized that Bloomfield's expressions 'non-distinctive' and 'no bearing whatsoever' have force only in the context of establishing a set of phonemes. The difference between my *l*-sounds is non-distinctive in so far as it does not require, in a conventional phonemic system based on the word, the setting up of two phonemes; it has very definite bearing in continuous speech when the final-type *l*-sound may occur in what is phonetically a non-final position, marking the end of a closely-knit group. The non-final type is found at the end of the word *fail* in the sentence *If I fail in May, I shall try again*

90

in December, but the final type appears, though there is no pause, in *If I fail, I shall try again in December*.

In a paper recently read to the Philological Society, my colleague A. E. Sharp drew attention to a number of distinctions that would escape notice if we simply relied on a phonemic transcription. It is well to remember with Sweet that we cannot tell *a priori* what sound-distinctions are significant in a language, and it is essential that we should constantly come back to the living language. It is probable that more work has been done on the phonetics of English than of any other language, but there is always more to learn.

There is indeed no end in sight to the need for further knowledge in any branch of the subject, and it must be a first concern of phoneticians in the universities to extend this knowledge and to train others to do so. The work will follow the two main lines of the phonetic and phonological description of particular languages and the development of general phonetic theory. The two cannot, of course, be divorced, though the special interests of any one worker may lead him particularly in one direction or the other. In terms of general phonetics, we need to know much more than we do about how the sound of speech is produced, and we also need to know much more than we do about how we respond to the sound waves that reach our ears during speech. Anatomy, physiology, psychology, physics, are all relevant to our problems, and the development of electronic equipment has opened the way to new lines of experimental research that must be fully exploited, though we have not exhausted the usefulness of our older experimental techniques, such as kymography and palatography.

The work must always be based on linguistic considerations, and it is from the study of particular languages that questions that are fully meaningful for the subject arise. When we consider how much work remains to be done in the phonetics of the more fully described languages such as English, we may well be both awed and inspired by the thought of the number that await even the beginnings of adequate description. The study of both the better known and the less well known will bring to light new questions for general phonetics, while the improvement of our techniques of phonetic description will have its effect on the phonologies established for particular languages. Professor Bazell found it necessary to say that, in phonology, linguists tend to diverge in their criteria of relevance, so that a feature that is present in the material for one is for the other virtually non-existent, and he added that the overall picture was one of scholars in strife over what the material is or should be. This is not necessarily an unhealthy situation, but it is assuredly one that calls for more and better phonetics. It arises partly from the divorce of phonetician and phonologist, but also from the fact that the material is extremely complex, and that it is possible to go quite a long way while ignoring some features. This cannot be satisfactory in the long run, and, as the means of handling them is developed, they must take their due place. The importance of intonation to the grammarian is now recognized, but we have scarcely begun on the study of voice quality, though it is certainly of great importance, not only as a special feature of some languages but in general terms for all.

It is not unusual to hear critics express their disbelief in work based on the observation of a single speaker. I think there is some misunderstanding here. In beginning to investigate a language that has not so far been described, a phonetician will work with one informant, and often enough publish the results of this work. This is partly a practical matter, since there may not be other speakers of the language readily available, and there is no reason to postpone a beginning simply on that account. But no phonetician will be ultimately satisfied with one informant, or think that he has described the language in dealing with him; he is probably more aware than most of the extent of individual variation. Nevertheless, the starting-point must necessarily be the study of one speaker. What we call the language is an abstraction based on observation of the habits of many individuals, but it is not a simple matter of statistics. Every speaker is different and works in terms of his own system as a whole. What we have to aim at is the statement of a system for the language to which we can relate all the individual systems of those who can be considered members of the speech community.

It is only when the system of a particular speaker has been established that valid comparison can begin, for the question is not simply whether, for example, he uses a tongue-tip trill or a uvular trill, but the part a particular feature plays within the system. When it comes to comparison, the statement will certainly have to be modified, and at later stages short-cuts become possible, but we are not at liberty to begin by taking something from one speaker and something from another.

It is of course prudent to assure oneself that one's informant is not markedly abnormal. But even if it subsequently appears that he had what is called a speech defect, the work in itself is not invalidated, for the speech defect has its place in the speaker's system, and, if he is an efficient member of his community as he obviously can be, it will be possible to relate it to the system set up for the language as a whole. It would certainly be wrong to take such a pronunciation as a model for teaching, but that is quite a different question.

No one who deals with language can avoid concerning him-self in some measure with phonetic matters, and anyone working on a hitherto undescribed or inadequately described language must of necessity act in the capacity of a phonetician for part of his time. It is clear that not all the work that is to be done can be carried out by what I will call professional phoneticians. Much excellent work, of significance for the subject as a whole, has been, and always will be, done by persons who are only part-time phoneticians working in relative isolation, but there is also a great deal of indifferent, not to say frankly bad, phonetics in the world. A university department brings together a group of highly-trained workers, who, devoting their lives to the subject, have time and opportunity to gain wide experience and, what is most important, to discuss its fundamental problems. It is a major function of these departments to act as centres that can, directly and indirectly, influence the work of the great number of people who make use of phonetics in some shape or form.

It is, I believe, essential that there should be a group, and that a university phonetician should not be working in isolation from his colleagues. Apart from the fact that his work tends to be dominated by the need to produce immediate answers for practical purposes, the part-time phonetician is usually at a disadvantage in lacking the facilities for the constant and easy consultation and exchange of information that is so necessary. A department of phonetics makes it possible for its members to form a team, each contributing from his special interests to the general discipline. If they were dispersed among a number of language departments, the advancement of the subject in the university, and the influence of the university on the outside world in its respect, would be greatly diminished. For the same reason, it would be very regrettable if a university were to rest content with the appointment of a single lecturer in phonetics. Isolation is wasteful and frustrating.

There is clearly a considerable advantage in having a group concerned with the training of future phoneticians, since it can provide for them the benefit of much wider experience than would otherwise be available and the stimulus of differing points of view. Anyone wishing to become a phonetician must develop his phonetic skill by work with as wide a range of languages as possible, for without the special skill as well as

94

knowledge he will be no phonetician. If, as Bloomfield warns, there is a danger that skill may lead to preoccupation with data without regard to its significance, there is equally a danger that lack of skill will lead to mere playing with letters.

The provision for the future and the continuity of development of the subject is an obvious responsibility, on which I need hardly dwell, and I turn to the other categories of students for whom phonetics is to be recommended as a part of their studies in the university.

To anyone concerned with the description of a living spoken language, whether he is a general linguist or a specialist in a particular language or group of languages, phonetics is indispensable, and the only question is whether it is to be good phonetics or not. It is, for example, impossible to give a full account of the grammar of spoken English without taking into account intonation and other features. If I say *it's too hot to eat this pudding* the meaning is different from that of the other sentence *it's too hot to eat, this pudding*. The words are the same, and no break is necessary in either, but the characteristic rhythm and intonation of each clearly distinguishes them. Similarly, the two sentences with the same words, *it isn't bad, is it*, would occur in quite different circumstances.

Even in historical linguistics, in which phonetics, lacking its material, has no direct place, phonetic knowledge has a definite bearing. It has a part to play in the interpretation of contemporary descriptions of old pronunciations and in keeping speculation about ancient pronunciations within the limits of probability. We know how much is concealed by even what is called a phonetic orthography, and there is no reason to suppose that things have ever been different in this respect. It is well to be aware of the kind of information that may be lacking when one examines a text, ancient or modern, from a linguistic point of view.

95

There are gifted people with what is called a good ear who can train themselves to do useful phonetic work, but their number is probably very small. Experience shows that most people need specific instruction, and that their powers of phonetic observation can in most cases be considerably improved by the application of well-tried methods of ear-training and exercises in articulatory control. Even with the help of gramophone records, phonetics can scarcely be studied from books; the peculiar nature of its material makes direct contact of teacher and student more essential than it is in most subjects. Even after training, phonetic skill varies from one person to another, and it is a very important aspect of such training that the student is put in the way of knowing with some precision how far he can rely on his own observations and in just what respects he is liable to error. The development of special skill is, of course, only one aspect of the matter, though one for which a teacher is of particular importance. It is also necessary for the student to learn how to handle the results of his observations, and it is likely that he will be saved a good deal of wasted time and effort if he receives formal teaching in the first place.

It would seem, then, reasonable to urge that phonetics should be a normal part of the basic preparation of all those who propose to undertake any form of linguistic research. It is unlikely that the time will prove to have been wasted for anyone, and few can dispense with it if they are to do the best work possible.

The kind of training must naturally vary with the purpose for which it is required. For those who are going to be engaged on phonetic research, it will need to be intensive, and will be given most appropriately at the postgraduate stage, the student working for a higher degree or postgraduate diploma. There is, however, a proper place for phonetics in undergraduate studies, and I point out that in the University of Edinburgh it

96

is one of the subjects that may be offered for the first, general degree, and is in fact offered by considerable numbers of students.

Any student of languages at a university, and I certainly do not exclude those whose interest is dominantly literary, would do well to learn something of the principles and methods of contemporary general linguistics, if only to be able to criticize them intelligently. Linguistics, in fact, already appears in the syllabus of a number of language degrees of this university. Whether the others should require an examination in the subject is a separate matter that I am not concerned to discuss here, but it would seem to me that a language specialist going down from the university at the present day without some knowledge of what is going on in general linguistics is in some danger of provincialism. But concern with language goes far beyond the traditional language departments at the present time; philosophers, psychologists, anthropologists, educationists, communications engineers, all find themselves involved. If a naïve and amateurish attitude to linguistic problems is to be avoided in their work, it seems clear that students of these subjects should be given some teaching in linguistics, so that they may at least be aware of the pitfalls that abound. A course for this purpose would necessarily include phonetics, for it is not possible to gain a real insight into linguistics without an acquaintance with the phonetics that is at its base, and we know that phonetic knowledge cannot be taken for granted. Undergraduates have little spare time, but, as I have remarked, phonetics lends itself less readily to private study than most subjects.

The question of what kinds of course to provide for the various categories of students is not altogether simple. Phonetics would not be suitable for a single-subject honours degree. This is not the occasion for discussing the desirability of instituting one in general linguistics, and I need only say that, if one were instituted, phonetics would undoubtedly have a very important place in the syllabus.

I need not go into details about the needs of those who are preparing themselves as phoneticians in the full sense of the word; their course must obviously be as extensive and as intensive as possible. It is, as always, the case of those who have least time to devote to the subject that presents the greatest difficulty.

There is almost everything to be said for approaching the subject through a particular language, not necessarily, and in some ways preferably not, the student's own; for it is in certain respects more difficult to begin with the phonetics of one's own language. With this, a student commonly has a preliminary difficulty in the need to overcome prepossessions that are likely to be more intractable than those he has with regard to a foreign language. He is apt to be unduly influenced by the spelling and by notions of correctness that he unwittingly fails to put into practice in his normal habits. These are facts of experience that have to be reckoned with. Again, for the purposes of an introductory class, it is easier to circumscribe the field in dealing with a foreign language, since, for this, attention can, for the time being, be restricted to one main kind of speech. In a class in which students are studying the phonetics of their own language, there will immediately come to light a considerable number of personal and dialectal differences, as well as complications due to differences of style, and it would be unsatisfactory and unsatisfying to leave these on one side even for the moment. Conditions of this sort are admirable at the right stage, but it must be allowed that they do not make things simpler for beginners. The common assumption that it is easier to study the phonetics of one's own language probably arises from the confusion of phonetics with learning to pronounce a new language. In point of fact, however, the conscious efforts of a student to pronounce the

98

language, and the mistakes he makes, can be a help to understanding its phonetics that is not available to him in quite the same way when he is studying the phonetics of his own language. In this last case, no one kind of pronunciation could be prescribed as correct, for the kind of course of which I am speaking is not concerned with normative work. In any case, most people would find it easier to make the gross changes that are required for the pronunciation of a new language than the comparatively subtle ones needed for a different variety of their own.

These are considerations that must be borne in mind in the planning of courses, but they are not decisive, and there are, of course, advantages in dealing with the student's mother-tongue, since the material is, so to speak, part of himself, and, once the possible early difficulties are overcome, readily available as a whole, so that reference may be made to any part of the material at any time, without the need to wait for some particular feature to appear at its due place in the exposition. In any event, it is not possible, in an English university, to do without constant illustration from English, though it clearly cannot be assumed that English will be the mother-tongue of all or even most of the students.

The great advantage of approaching the study of phonetics through a particular language is that in doing so one is working with a whole, and it is possible to refer each item to its place in a system, so that its real significance may be appreciated, and one of the dangers to which Bloomfield called attention avoided. A student reading modern languages cannot well dispense with a study of the phonetics of the languages of his choice. Without this, it seems to me, he is not fully equipped. He is in the position of someone who writes and speaks correctly but knows nothing about the grammar. If the aim is simply to acquire proficiency for practical purposes, this is entirely unobjectionable, but such an aim is scarcely sufficient for a student of languages at a university.

Ideally, all students of phonetics should, at some stage, make a study of the phonetics of at least one language, but this is not always practically possible, because of lack of time on their part as well as the difficulty of providing the large number of courses that would probably be needed. In practice, students whose other occupations are of various kinds, often not linguistic, must often be grouped together for their work in phonetics, and no one language may be suitable. The language background of the members of the class is likely to vary, and those who will be unable to proceed to other courses will need a wider survey. For these, it is necessary to provide courses in general phonetics.

Even when the introductory course is based on one language, general phonetics must obviously take a large place in it, since it provides the means of describing and classifying the features of the phonic material, but the method of presentation and the emphasis on special features will be determined by the language studied. In a general course, the aim must be to show the principles of description and classification by reference to examples drawn from many languages and showing features of as many kinds as possible. The danger to be guarded against is too uncritical a concern with phenomena and an impression that there are such things as separate speech sounds. It is thus necessary to take every opportunity of showing how one feature may be related to other features of an utterance in a way that will vary from one language to another. The discussion of the principles of notation will be involved as well as an introduction to the problems of phonology. In the circumstances of a course of this kind, only limited problems can be dealt with, and they must be chosen with care for the light they throw on general principles.

Without practical work, a course in phonetics loses a great

deal of its value, and provision must be made for it whenever possible, though it is not always easy to arrange because of the many demands on a student's time. But even when it has to be reduced to a minimum, I believe the courses to be valuable. The students in an introductory class will not emerge as trained, but they can be given an insight into the aims and methods of phonetics, and at least come to know what is involved in the making of a phonetic description.

I turn finally to a question of applied phonetics, the teaching of pronunciation. To acquire a good pronunciation of a foreign language is an essentially practical matter, and provided the pronunciation is good, or at least acceptable, it does not greatly matter how it is acquired. In teaching it, any trick that will produce the required result is justified. The first line of attack, though it is not very often sufficient, must always be to provide a model for imitation, but, as might be expected, when teaching has to be carried beyond this, it is most often successful, and most successful, when it is based on accurate phonetic knowledge. The best results are likely when the teacher not only knows that a mistake is being made but just how it is being made, so that he may devise means of working from the incorrect articulation to what is required. But, in the practical matter of dealing with pronunciation, this knowledge is for the teacher rather than the pupil. When, as not infrequently happens, someone tells me that he was taught phonetics at school, I am inclined to think that this would have been misguided if it were true. It is the teaching of pronunciation not the teaching of phonetics that is important in schools.

There is no doubt that the standard of the pronunciation of foreign languages has greatly improved with the diffusion of phonetic knowledge, but a good deal of lip-service is still paid to phonetics, and there is a good deal of real but not well-informed enthusiasm. It is, for example, still depressingly often necessary to point out that the letters of the International

Phonetic Alphabet can do nothing by themselves for anyone's pronunciation, that they only serve to tell a pupil when to use sounds he has already learned. They can be very useful, properly handled, but they are not phonetics, and they are by no means indispensable in the teaching of pronunciation. What is required for that is sound phonetic knowledge on the part of the teacher.

A language teacher, whether in school or university, has, it would seem to me, a clear responsibility for his students' pronunciation, and he should be no less well able to deal with this than with the rest of his teaching. Though it will not normally fall to him to teach phonetics as such, he must himself have had sufficient phonetic training for his purpose. It is not merely a matter of classroom techniques, and his phonetic studies should not be left to the time when he receives his training as a teacher. Departments of education should be able to assume that he comes not only with sufficient knowledge of his languages in other respects, but with adequate phonetic knowledge too.

It is for the phonetician to give the training that is needed by the language teacher, but the teaching of pronunciation is not in itself one of his primary duties. His business is to teach phonetics, and it is only incidentally to this that he is concerned with the practical matter of modifying his students' pronunciation. In point of fact, however, when he is dealing with the phonetics of a particular language he will be greatly concerned with this side of things. His training specially fits him for it, and no phonetician can happily tolerate anything short of the best performance his students are capable of producing. Living speech is his material, and he knows that it must be treated with the greatest respect.

The Study of the Present-day English Language: A Triple Bond Between Disciplines

An inaugural lecture delivered on 19 November 1962 by
P. D. STREVENS, *Professor of Contemporary English in the University of Leeds*

The Study of the Present-day English Language: a Triple Bond Between Disciplines

The creation of a new Chair, with a unique title, is an event certain to arouse comment and speculation. The first incumbent of the Chair has a clear duty to satisfy this speculation by stating what the nature of his subject really is, and how he seeks to profess it; and that is what I hope to achieve in this lecture. In so doing, I hope also to show that this is a proper and natural development from the existing range of English studies pursued with such vigour and distinction at Leeds, and finally to indicate the relations which exist between studies in Contemporary English and in certain other university disciplines.

What, then, is meant by 'Contemporary English'? I must begin by saying that this is a label, not a technical term. It is not the name of a single, self-evident subject, but rather a convenient label to refer to some particular branches of English studies, reinforced by the attitudes and techniques of modern linguistic thought. The label has been used increasingly in recent years, and there is at least one important and distinguished piece of research fundamental to this grouping of subjects: I am referring to Professor Randolph Quirk's *Survey of Contemporary English Usage*, upon the results of which will be based a new and authoritative description of English grammar as evidenced in the speech and writing of educated people at the present time.

The scope of the Chair of Contemporary English likewise embraces new grammatical descriptions, but it also ranges more widely than this. It includes two main kinds of work, each in a sense independent yet interlinked. They are, first, the study of the present-day language, and second, the study and teaching of English as a foreign language. I shall refer to these as the 'academic' and 'vocational' aspects respectively, of my work, and before describing them in detail I must make clear my view of the relations between them. The reputation of the new Chair will depend in the long run upon the academic programme of studies in Contemporary English. The vocational programme is an application of the theories and the attitudes of the academic work and of the data which will be derived from it, and although the vocational programme—the study and teaching of English as a foreign language—will often seem more spectacular, will attract more money from outside sources, and will seem to the public to be more obviously 'useful' in a short-term sense, nevertheless it is wholly dependent upon the academic programme. Without the academic, the vocational could not exist in terms acceptable to a university, since it would lack the essential strength of theory and of data which the academic study of Contemporary English can provide for it; whereas the academic programme itself has its own independent existence.

In order to describe the basic, academic side of this cluster of studies which we call Contemporary English, let us divide it into two main parts: first, the subject of study—the material with which we concern ourselves—and second, the methods used. Having done that we shall mention some of the research projects envisaged at Leeds.

The subject of study can be summarized as 'the present-day English language, in both written and spoken forms'. Those of us who were brought up at school on a diet of English grammar of the Nesfield or Lindley Murray type may wonder what is new or different in Contemporary English, and why it should be necessary to replace a body of doctrine that has existed for many years. The answer is that the descriptions of English language taught in most schools leave a great deal to be

106

desired, from four points of view. First, they are not *descriptions*, they are *prescriptions*: they state how (in the opinion of the grammarian) people ought to write English, not how people actually do so. Secondly, they are statements about only part of the language; about grammar and about some aspects of vocabulary (although some of the antiquarian items included under 'collective nouns' have no current existence outside school-books. I learn from a recently published school grammar, for instance, that the following are 'group terms or collectives': a baren of mules; a clowder of cats; a gang of elks; a rag of colts; a budget of papers; a caste of flower-pots). Thirdly, most school textbooks descriptions of English are not contemporary in what they purport to describe: they include a great deal that is out of date and they omit a great deal that is vital and living. And finally, they use a framework of description that works well for Greek and Latin but is less than perfect for English, since English is a different kind of language. Descriptions of Contemporary English will look very different from some of the textbooks we have been accustomed to.

But the simple and convenient summary of my subject, 'the present-day English language, in both written and spoken forms', masks a complexity that few of us appreciate until we attempt the task of describing English. This language called 'English' is not, in fact, one single, unified language, and when our school textbooks taught us what purported to be *the* rules of English they did us a poor service because they diverted our attention away from the fact that large numbers of different sub-languages of English co-exist. Naturally, by virtue of all being varieties of the same language, English, they share many common features, but they also display differences between them that are as illuminating as the similarities.

Contemporary English accepts every manifestation of the present-day language as being a fit subject for study; but it follows from this acceptance that a prior task presents itself, the task of studying the kinds of variation that exist within the language. We need to study *varieties* of English before we can study any single variety. Let us name some examples of different varieties of English: the written English of the Admiralty *Manual of Seamanship* is different from the English of motor-car insurance policies, or from a knitting pattern, or from a cookery book, or from a textbook on electronics. The spoken English of a commentary on a boxing match is different from that of a sermon. And both these sets of examples, spoken and written, would be different yet again if they originated in the United States of America rather than in Great Britain. Of course, everyone is aware from his own experience that differences exist between dialects, or accents, or styles, or fields of discourse: what is *not* universally realized is, first, that all these varieties are equally fit subjects for study—in other words, that we are not seeking some notional ideal of 'good English' which is to be described while all other kinds of English are to be ignored—and second, that we now have an effective framework of categories for analysing and describing the kinds of difference that occur.

Our awareness of this problem has greatly increased in the past three or four years. Those of us who study the present-day language are at last able to show the different dimensions whose interplay determines which variety of English is used by a given individual on any given occasion. There are several ways of approaching the study of varieties of English: in particular, one may either follow the lead of J. C. Catford and concentrate upon the performer (that is, the speaker or writer), in which case one relates the variety of English to his personal identity, where he comes from, his social status, his role in the situation, his relation to those he is addressing, and so on; or one may follow M. A. K. Halliday and concentrate upon the language itself, in which case one deals with the dialect, with the subject of the discourse, with speech as a different kind of event from writing, with different 'modes' within each (journalism, the formal lecture, diary-writing, and so on), and with the 'styles of discourse' that depend upon the relations between the participants in any piece of language. Either way, we can be rather detailed in our analysis, which allows us to pin down varieties of English in a precise manner.

This is a branch of Contemporary English that borders on sociology and anthropology, since the constraints upon the language of an individual are part of his learned behaviour and part of his total cultural patterns. This may seem a long way from the traditional tasks of describing the phonemes or the grammar or the lexis of a particular variety of English, but it is necessary just the same that a framework for describing varieties of English should be found in order that the particular variety being described should first be precisely identified.

Once we have selected a particular variety of present-day English for study, what do we include within our description of it? Before specifying the answer in detail we must first point out that the kind of description that emerges will be determined very largely by the theory of language accepted by the researcher. If you accept the orthodox views on American structural linguistics, then your description of English must come out rather like those of Trager and Smith, or A. A. Hill. If you prefer the more recent American views of grammar as a combination of generation and transformation, in the manner of Chomsky, then your description of English will probably come out like those of Stockwell or Roberts, or Lees. If your preference (like that of my colleagues and myself) is for the modern British outlook on linguistics—in particular, for that theory associated with the labels of 'the London School' or 'the Edinburgh School'—then you will produce a description of English rather like those of Quirk or Strang, or the eagerly-awaited but as yet unpublished descriptions by Catford, Halliday and Sinclair.[1]

Within the kind of description we propose there will be four main sections, which we shall call *phonology*, *grammar*, *lexis*, and *context*. The use of these terms is sufficiently close to their traditional currency for me to explain fairly simply what is meant. First, phonology. This is not quite the 'phonetics of English' of the traditional kind—that associated, for example, with the name of Professor Daniel Jones (under whom I had the privilege of working as a research student). Phonology starts with the same data but takes it to a further degree of abstraction. The phonology of a variety of English includes not simply the inventory of the speech-sounds used in it, but this inventory further analysed to show systematic groupings and to show all the functional units of sound, right up to the largest unit of all, the tone-group (that is, the intonation unit). And then in addition, a phonological statement includes the relations between these units. Thus, following M. A. K. Halliday, the phonology of that variety of English which I use (roughly Standard English as to grammar, R.P. as to accent) would describe a system of five *tone-groups*; each tone-group consists of one or more *feet*, one of which will be the 'tonic' foot; each foot consists of one or more *syllables*, which are each either stressed or weak; each syllable consists of one or more *phonemes*, which can occur only in certain permitted arrangements.[2]

[1] A full-scale bibliography of British work would be out of place here. Three publications, however, must be cited: M. A. K. Halliday, 'Categories of the Theory of Grammar', in *Word*, vol. xvii, no. 3 (December 1961); Randolph Quirk, *The Use of English* (Longmans, 1962); Barbara M. H. Strang, *Modern English Structures* (Arnold, 1962). Three important sets of working papers on Contemporary English Grammar have been in semi-private circulation, associated with the names of J. C. Catford, S. P. Corder, and J. McH. Sinclair. All the above works have contributed to the view of English grammar adopted in this lecture.

[2] This phonological analysis, which owes much to David Abercrombie, has the advantage that it incorporates the whole range of rhythmical, prosodic, and phonemic features of English in a single comprehensive statement.

I have deliberately gone into detail over phonology in order to show that it is based firmly and solely upon accurate and sophisticated observation of *phonetic* detail, while nevertheless not being identical with phonetics. Phonology is a level of language description intermediate between the basic, substantial data of phonetics on the one hand, and the more abstract patterns of grammar on the other. And the moral of this is that for making descriptions of English—or indeed, of any language—the worker needs a solid grounding in phonetics: not simply in the pronunciation of the language, but in the identification and classification of *all* sounds and sound-features, including those which occur in the particular variety of the language he is studying.

In addition to the phonology of the variety of English being studied, the description must include a statement of the *grammar*. (Under the heading of grammar we include all those phenomena which have traditionally been separated into *morphology* and *syntax*.) This level of language, too, is to be described in terms of the units of grammar found to occur (for example, sentence, clause, phrase or group, word, morpheme), the classes and sub-classes of each and the patterns of arrangement which they take up in structure, and the relations between the members of the hierarchy.

A statement must also be made of the *lexis* (that is, roughly, the vocabulary) of the variety of English being studied. Here we are interested not only in the items that occur (the words, groups of words, expressions) but in the company that each one keeps, in the co-occurrence of some words and the mutual exclusiveness of others. To take a trivial example, in the register of astronomy items like *star, planet, constellation* will almost certainly occur with considerable frequency; but the item *horoscope* will almost certainly not occur at all. In astrology, on the other hand, a different grouping will occur, in which *horoscope* and the names of the signs of the Zodiac *do* collocate with the other terms which we expect to find in astronomy. Of course, this is perfectly obvious, and the reason for producing an example is not to suggest that we can now talk about word-groupings where previously we could not; the reason is rather to suggest that our techniques for doing this now have greater precision, accuracy and delicacy than they previously displayed.

The task of description is nearly complete, once we have covered phonology, grammar, and lexis, but we still have to include a statement of the contextual features of the variety of English we are dealing with. We must state the circumstances under which this variety occurs, and any limiting or defining features, such as restriction to a particular subject (as with the word *horoscope*, for example), or occupation, or social class; or even a more restricted set of contexts such as those which define the language of detergent advertising, or newspaper headlines, or the instructions on the labels of fireworks.

These, then, are the components of a complete description of any variety of contemporary English: phonology, grammar, lexis, context. And all varieties of English in use today are fit subjects for study. One of our problems is that once our eyes are opened to the great range of varieties that exist, and once our prejudices are broken down to allow us to study any variety, not simply the conventional notion of what constitutes 'good English', we then also discover what an immense task of description lies before us.

There is one particular variety of English to which we must pay special attention, and that is the language of literature. The appreciation of literature and the evaluation of literary merit are activities with their own procedures and techniques which do not in general impinge on Contemporary English. But one aspect of the total study of literary texts is the detailed analysis of the language used in them, and of those linguistic devices which produce particular literary effects. This requires techniques of language analysis such as those employed by Contemporary English in other branches of its study. Here, then, is a real possibility of bridge-building, provided that we are clear from the outset that it is a joint effort, with the building proceeding simultaneously from both ends, and aimed at the same point in the middle. In other words, the specialist in contemporary language must work with and towards the specialist in literature, and the specialist in literature must work with and towards the language specialist.

It is worth stressing that those who attempt this task must be specialists. The field of Contemporary English has suffered from more than its fair share of well-meaning but ill-informed amateurs. Simply because one speaks the language there is no reason to suppose that one can produce, without further training, an insightful analysis of the complex interplay of patterns that make up our language.

For most people, it is only by experience, by training the sensibility, by learning the art of delicate discrimination, that insight into literature can become habitual. One kind of discrimination involved is the discrimination of the patterns of language; but this requires some detailed knowledge of what the patterns of language actually consist of, at all levels, and of how they interweave. Just as grammarians and specialists in linguistics are not automatically capable of making sensitive and illuminating statements about literary effect and artistic merit, so, too, the literary specialist if he expects his remarks about language to be of weight and worth, must find a basis of linguistic understanding.

The essential point is that there is an important area of overlap between language and literature. It is possible to carry out studies in literature without touching the linguistic aspects of creative writing; it is equally possible to carry out studies in Contemporary English without touching the language of literature. But for either discipline to be full and complete it must take notice of the other.

This area of overlap, which at Leeds we are calling Style and Rhetoric but which has often been labelled 'stylistics' (although that term has also been used for other, non-linguistic, studies), is one of our special preoccupations. It is a subject which has baffled many workers in the past, as it may possibly baffle us in the future, but we believe that we are better equipped now to tackle the inter-disciplinary collaboration than previous generations may have been. The reasons for this are worth attempting to convey.

Descriptions of English until recently have been largely *prescriptive*, they have been related to the written language, and they have used categories of description borrowed from Latin, not based on a general theory. This made it difficult to describe any other kind of English than the particular prescriptive model of written prose that was the subject of conventional grammatical description, since no adequate descriptive categories existed for other kinds of written English, or for any kind of speech. Yet it is precisely in literature that the linguistic patterns are at their most subtle and sophisticated, where the levels of sound, grammar, and lexis interpenetrate in the most complex and original ways. Our newer descriptions of English will at least remove this serious methodological impediment, since we believe them to be capable of embracing any and all of the possible patterns and variations of the language. There remains a whole set of relations between the literary text and the linguistic statement—relations of genre, argument, intent, and other devices—for which no adequate framework of description yet exists. This is the vineyard in which my colleague Mr John Spencer is labouring. The omens for the grape-harvest are good: with luck we may even produce a vintage, but do not expect the wine to mature too quickly.

One further area of study deserves to be mentioned, and that is the extension of English studies into the realm of the mass media of communication. This is a *terrain vague*, in the sense that it is new, undefined, and not obviously the responsibility of any single discipline. It is related to education, to sociology, to literature, and drama, to journalism, and to language. Contemporary English obviously has an interest here, although not an exclusive interest.

We come now to the methods of study appropriate to Contemporary English. These methods rest upon the two disciplines sometimes called 'the linguistic sciences', namely, *phonetics* and *linguistics*.[1] By 'linguistics' in this context I mean, above all, a theory of language: an understanding of how language works. With this theory and the descriptive categories which it imposes we can describe any form of spoken or written English, and we can relate it to all other aspects of language behaviour. Naturally, in the course of describing English one hopes to go further and to analyse grammar, lexis or phonology to a deeper level of detail, or 'delicacy'; and this entails a close knowledge of the particular structures and systems that operate in the present-day language. But these are in a sense extra to the first requisite, which is a theory of language, and an understanding of how language works, of how all languages work.

Let us be quite clear that I am using the word *theory* not in the conversational way in which it is generally employed in the humanities, to mean a supposition, or a hunch, or an impression; I am using it as a technical term from general scientific

---

[1] For me, linguistics presupposes phonetics. In order to describe any language completely we must have techniques for handling the spoken form of that language; and for those areas of speech that are not grammatical or lexical in nature, it is phonetics that supplies the necessary techniques. Phonetics, of course, has other sides to it, and indeed, it has a viable existence as an academic discipline quite apart from its contribution to descriptive linguistics. The point is that phonetics is an indispensable component of linguistics, and therefore my references to linguistics will henceforward assume the inclusion of phonetics as may be relevant.

method. When I say that we need a theory of language, I mean a group of abstractions derived from the observation of facts and embodying all those hypotheses about the nature of language that have been found valid. And out of the theory come the descriptive categories and relationships which the theory specifies for language in general. This has a profound effect upon our description of a particular language, since it means that we are describing a language in its own terms, using only those categories which it is necessary to invoke because they reflect the way the language operates.[1]

In defining the field of Contemporary English I acknowledged that it is not a single subject but a grouping of some branches of English studies. But there is nevertheless a unity in the grouping: the underlying similarity shared by all the varied aspects of Contemporary English that I am describing springs from the sharing of a comprehensive theory of language. Every one of the teaching and research projects in Contemporary English begun or now being planned, both at Leeds and in other British universities, has as its basis this outlook on language.

At this point we may conveniently look at the projects which we envisage for Contemporary English at this university. One essential piece of development is in the field of grammar. Our frequent need to describe this level of the language to undergraduate and postgraduate students is at present frustrated by the paucity of grammatical descriptions in acceptable terms. Those who work in Contemporary English, not only at Leeds but in other universities, are engaged in the slow, reduplicative task of observing, analysing, classifying, describing; we are gradually writing our own new grammars of Contemporary English, and this process will continue for some years. It is one of our major tasks, but the least spectacular.

[1] The present holder of the Chair of Comparative Philology in the University of Cambridge, Professor W. Sidney Allen, has dealt in full and lucid detail with this question in his Inaugural Lecture, entitled *On the Linguistic Study of Languages*.

We are interested, too, in phonological problems, especially in the interpenetration of phonology and grammar. Everyone knows from his own experience that changes of intonation (to take a simple instance) can carry changes of a grammatical kind, as in the difference between *He's coming on Friday?* and *He's coming on Friday.* There are a great many other relations between these two levels, which few people have studied in detail.[1] At Leeds we have been fortunate in securing funds from the University Grants Committee to purchase some of the more complex equipment in the field of acoustic phonetics which will be needed for studies of this kind, and we look forward to the development of research in collaboration with the Phonetics Department.

Another basic project which is already under way concerns the relations between language and context. Here we are back once again close to the point where we began, namely, the study of different varieties of English, since some of the choices between possible alternative forms of English are determined by features of the context. Mr S. P. Corder is investigating this question and has begun by a preliminary study of the language used in highly restricted situations. One situation he chose was a tobacconist's shop, where throughout most of a working day he sat and observed the forms of language used there. It became quite clear (as indeed we should anticipate, if we gave thought to it) that the precise language used was not the same for all speakers, but was divided into a small number of types, selected according to the relations between the customer and the shopkeeper. The analysis of total situations and of the language used in them is a difficult problem but one which we shall attempt to reduce for the light it throws upon

---

[1] One notable exception is Professor Randolph Quirk, whose paper, *The correspondence of prosodic to grammatical features in spoken English*, presented to the Ninth International Congress of Linguists in August 1962, points the way to a wide range of further investigations.

language behaviour as a whole, and upon the complex, inter-locking patterns of varieties of English.

In the field of lexis we are driven to make statements about the patterns of occurrence and co-occurrence of words and other lexical items in very large samples of text. This is a statistical operation for which certain computer techniques are very well suited. Thanks to the offer of computer facilities, both by Dr P. Wexler at Manchester and Dr G. B. Cook at Leeds, we hope to mount a large-scale lexical study, working with texts of both spoken and written language, amounting to several million running words.

To sum up, our programme in Contemporary English must include research and investigation in all areas of the language. We have made a start and will extend as staff and finance permit. This is not simply a pious statement of intent: on the contrary, our teaching programme lacks some of the basic data, so that we are driven by the pressure of our day-to-day teaching to investigate as widely and yet as deeply as we can the nature of the present-day language. Fortunately we are not alone: other universities (notably London and Edinburgh) already have programmes of the same general kind, and much mutual consultation and catalysis takes place.

As to teaching, we have begun this term to offer a new alternative syllabus for the B.A. Degree in Special Studies, English. This syllabus combines literature and language with some study of Style and Rhetoric. In addition to the normal language work in their first year, undergraduates following this Modern English syllabus take phonetics, linguistics, and the description of the present-day language. Similar courses, at a more advanced level, are offered in some of our postgraduate schemes of study.

Leeds is, of course, an appropriate site for advanced studies in language not only because it is Leeds, but also because it is in Yorkshire. One of the greatest figures in British linguistics, the late Professor J. R. Firth, was a Yorkshireman and proud of it; while one of his most influential pupils, Dr Michael Halliday, is not only a Yorkshireman, but is also the son of our own Dr Wilfrid Halliday, the collaborator with Professor Orton in the Dialect Survey. Indeed, the University itself was clearly ready for new undertakings in the field of language at the time it decided to create the Chair I have the honour to occupy. Professor Orton's distinguished work on English dialects (now, happily, in the early stages of publication); Professor Ullmann's world-wide eminence in the field of semantics; one of the oldest departments of Phonetics in the country; a university Linguistics Society; linguistic interests in Psychology, in Philosophy and in Education; and above all the concept of a wide-ranging School of English, achieved by the vision of Professor A. N. Jeffares, containing not only the usual studies in literature and philology, but also less common branches of English Studies: Celtic and Icelandic, American and Commonwealth literature, and Folk-life Studies; these were some of the features existing in Leeds that made this development, in its academic aspects alone, natural and easy. Other favourable features existed on the applied or vocational side, which we shall shortly consider.

I have dwelt at length upon the academic content of Contemporary English because it stands in its own right as a respectable and rapidly expanding branch of university studies. It exists independently of any practical applications and would continue even if there were no demand for applied or vocational programmes. But such a demand does exist, on a very large scale; and since it is backed by sources of money over and above the University's own funds, since the demand in many cases has the further sanction of the national interest and international collaboration, and since we know how to ensure that our academic work is encouraged and fed, not stifled and starved by the outside pressures: for all these reasons the

University very properly intends to meet the demand by building up a centre for the study and teaching of English as a foreign language. Contemporary English supplies to this work the background of linguistic thought and the necessary description of present-day English, while the teacher-training and educational components are supplied by the Department and the Institute of Education.

Let us look more closely at the contribution of Contemporary English on the vocational or applied side. In recent years the number of people learning English and using English for various purposes, but not speaking it as their mother tongue, has grown to an astronomical size. Estimates vary around the figure of two hundred million overseas users of English, with great diversity of quantity, quality and motives in their use of the language. By far the most urgent set of problems, naturally, relates to the teaching of English to this vast population; but to forestall the hasty conclusion that the function of Contemporary English is training overseas teachers of English, it is necessary to make two points: first, these are by no means the only problems; and second, our contribution lies elsewhere than in the area of classroom methods, educational theory and normal pedagogical training.

We can contribute, for example, in the field of Institutional Linguistics (to use the term coined some years ago by Mr John Spencer), which deals with the difficult technical problems of national language policy in multilingual countries. We are able to integrate this with various of our academic studies: with our view of the nature of language as a social phenomenon; with our study of varieties of English (which by definition include varieties outside Great Britain); with our analysis of problems of English overseas, of language contact, of bilingualism. These are matters of consuming importance in many countries in Africa and Asia, but they are also highly technical matters, where ignorance, prejudice and amateurism can do great harm.

It may help us to see why these are such vital questions if we consider some of the functions of English in Africa. First, English is often the only feasible language of internal political unity. A country like Nigeria, for example, with three Regions, each having a different economic basis, a different cultural pattern, different political aims and different indigenous languages, needs as the administrative and political link between its dissimilar parts a language free from local partisanship. English supplies this link. In the second place, African states throughout the continent need a means of collaborating with each other: English and French supply that means, where no single African language is at present acceptable. And in the third place, Africa as a whole seeks a window on world civilization: once again it is English and French that serve this purpose (except for North Africa, which is part of Islam and hence uses Arabic). In other words, the function of English is no longer a direct product of the political and social system of Great Britain, it has purposes which are far more immediate and localized, independently of Britain.

There are those who say that the change in the functions of English abroad need not concern us; but this is to ignore reality. The demand for expert advice, professional collaboration, and schemes of specialist training, comes spontaneously from the countries with the problems. (Indeed, one of the major practical problems of a Professor of Contemporary English is dealing with the great flood of requests for professional advice and assistance that washes in with every post!) And although the demand is often directed towards Britain in the first instance, help will be accepted by these countries from almost any quarter. To meet this demand, the United States has a massive programme of specialist aid to Africa and Asia in the field of English; France has entered the business of teaching English and does so by methods that are both intensive and effective; even the Soviet Union contributes in various ways to meet this same demand for English. Britain cannot hold back; and what we propose at Leeds, together with similar plans in the other university centres currently in this field—London, Edinburgh, Manchester, and Bangor—constitutes the university component of the national response.

But where, precisely, does Contemporary English enter into this programme? Is it not simply a matter of supplying more English teachers to schools overseas; or at the highest is it not just a teacher-training problem, best solved by improving the training colleges in the countries concerned? These courses of action are necessary and can make a useful contribution, but they are not the only ways of helping, and they are certainly not the best way for British universities to assist. Our main contribution in Britain is of three kinds: first, giving academic and professional training to university and training-college staff from the countries concerned so that they can raise the standards of their own institutions when they return home; second, preparing British graduates as university staff and trainers of teacher-trainers; and third, providing the best possible academic content for these courses of professional training and their overseas counterparts. It is the third of these sub-divisions that is the most relevant to our own interests in Contemporary English here at Leeds.

At this point we approach a delicate question of doctrine in the matter of teaching foreign languages. It will be obvious that the problems of English as a foreign language are fundamentally similar to those of French as a foreign language, or Russian, or Chinese, and until comparatively recently the attitudes and techniques used by British teachers going abroad to teach English were similar to, and even based upon, the older, more conventional attitudes towards teaching foreign languages in this country which were current before the War. Similar methods used to be current in the United States, until America reached a point of crisis, during the War. They were faced with a sudden need to teach practical language ability in English and in several other languages to immigrants and to soldiers; they decided that conventional methods were not efficient or effective enough for the purpose, and so they cast around for other means.

Out of this operation, reinforced by a traumatic reaction to the launching of the first Russian satellite, there emerged in the United States an attitude towards language teachers which said, approximately, 'Make them good structural linguists and the problem will be solved.' This point of view was widely held for a number of years. In Britain, on the other hand, at roughly the same period, the converse doctrine held sway: 'Make them good teachers, and the problem will be solved.' It is now clear to most people that neither of these exclusive attitudes is the best solution. It turned out, on the American side, that only those linguists who were also good teachers could make really effective use of the sophisticated linguistic materials they were given to teach with; while on the British side, even the best classroom teachers were handicapped by the rudimentary linguistics which underlay much of the teaching material used. In the nineteen-sixties, both attitudes have been modified. Some American institutions are increasing the methodology component of their courses, while some British professional training courses are illuminating their admirable methodology with a sound linguistic background. The point of this sketchy and compressed summary of recent history in teaching English is that it shows the genesis of our own outlook at Leeds, which is that there must be a marriage of the two components.

In other words, the teaching of English as a foreign language has become a joint activity, containing on the one hand both education and methodology (which are most properly provided, as at Leeds, by the specialists in Education), and on the other hand a sound background of linguistic thought and up-to-date descriptions of the present-day language (which are properly provided by the specialists in language and in English). There may well be some overlap in functions: this is largely a question of the number of specialist staff that any given institution can afford; but the principle is clear.

The particular projects which Leeds is building in this domain and to which Contemporary English contributes are of three main kinds. First, there are the professional qualifications which teachers of English overseas can take, and which involve collaboration between the School of English, the Department of Education and the Institute of Education. To be precise, at the present time there are offered the Postgraduate Diploma in English Studies (designed chiefly for overseas students) and the Postgraduate Diploma in English as a Second Language (designed mainly for graduates of British Isles universities); the Diploma in English as a Second Language can be taken in the form of a Joint Course between Contemporary English and the Department of Education for those who wish to acquire training as a teacher in addition to the specialist content from Contemporary English. There are plans for a new Certificate in the Teaching of English as a Foreign Language to be offered in the Institute of Education to overseas students, especially from Africa, for which the specialist material on language and on English would be provided by Contemporary English.

Then there are longer-term proposals for links with university centres overseas, in America, Africa, and Asia. These links, when they can be achieved, will enable the countries which have problems of this kind to benefit in their own vocational programmes from the fruits of the academic side of Contemporary English at Leeds. In addition, they should give practical expression to the ideal (much talked-of but rarely achieved) of collaboration in this field between Britain and America.

The third kind of project concerns the development of mass

media and technical aids for teaching purposes. Just as stylistics is an area in the academic programme where Contemporary English overlaps with another branch of English studies, to their mutual enrichment, so also there is an area in the vocational programme where Contemporary English overlaps with the pedagogical arts. It is no accident that specialists in Contemporary English should everywhere be called upon to assist in the exploitation of television, radio, language, laboratories, audio-visual aids, and teaching machines, for the purposes of teaching English. It is simply a reflection of the fact that these devices by themselves, effective though they may be in principle, are of little use unless they are programmed by specialists in language and in English. This is how one of my colleagues comes to be not only a specialist in the grammar of the present-day language but also a leading expert in the use of television for educational purposes; and this also is how we come to be consulted in the development of language laboratories and audio-visual methods. Our interest is not in the devices themselves, nor in the art of teaching, but in the fact that without our specialist contribution these devices cannot effectively do the job that is asked of them.

We are called in, then, by those who teach English as a foreign language, to provide the theoretical basis and the best possible description of English, as part of the total language-teaching job. But the profession of teaching English as a foreign language is only one particular case of the general category of teaching foreign languages; and to the extent that teaching English as a foreign language can be shown to have improved in effectiveness by the marriage of our theory and description with the best possible teaching methods and techniques, to that extent we are likely to arouse the interest of those who teach foreign languages other than English. This explains the links that have spontaneously arisen between modern-language teaching and Contemporary English. It is certainly not the case that we are attempting to show our modern-language colleagues in the schools how to do their job—on the contrary, we have much to learn from them—but simply that the teaching of English as a foreign language has recently gone through a revolution of aims, methods and techniques, a revolution that contains many parallels for foreign-language teaching.

Let me mention a single example: there is at present in Britain a wave of interest in the teaching of foreign languages in the primary schools.[1] New social and political pressures make it virtually certain that before long some European languages will be taught to *all* children, and from an early age, instead of only to a small proportion of children, late in their school career, as at present. But to many teachers this is a dangerous experiment: 'Who knows', many of them ask, 'whether young children *can* learn languages, without suffering ing psychological harm?' The answer is that some of those who teach English as a foreign language know, because they have been doing it for years in Africa and elsewhere.

There is yet a further extension of these collaborations. Many of those who teach English language in schools in Britain are unhappy about the aims and syllabuses of their profession, and about the textbooks they have to use. It is a remarkable fact that a number of textbooks designed to describe the present-day English language to foreign learners have suddenly begun to sell in quantity at home. Two trends seem to be at work, as far as one can judge: first, many teachers are seeking descriptions of English that relate to the way it is actually used, in speech and writing, today; and there are few works that meet this specification. And second, many teachers

[1] Incidentally, Leeds leads in the exploitation of this possibility. The city's Chief Education Officer, Mr George Taylor, has pioneered several experiments along these lines, including the famous scheme taught by Mrs Kellermann. No other area in Britain has done so much.

want to present a description that rests on a coherent framework of theory and description. Here we are back at my starting-place, the academic study of the present-day language; but the point I am making is that Contemporary English can contribute to the teaching of English as a foreign language, to the teaching of foreign languages in general, and to the teaching of English in Britain.

Just as it was natural that an academic programme combining the study of language and the study of English should arise in Leeds at the present time, so also it is natural that the vocational programme should do so. Quite apart from the close interest that our Vice-Chancellor has always displayed in the problems of overseas territories, a number of other factors were propitious. The British Council, whose policy in this field has been outstandingly clear-sighted, gave the University a strong injection of financial support and helped in several other ways. A high proportion of the staff of the School of English have overseas experience, including Professor A. N. Jeffares (whose drive and foresight are responsible for the establishment of the entire scheme) and Dr Charles Barber, who has taken charge of the Diploma in English Studies (that is, the Diploma mainly for overseas students) since it began in 1957; and indeed, many of the staff of the School of English have worked in the field of English studies abroad, and have encountered most of the practical problems that arise. Naturally one should beware of equating too closely the teaching of literature in European countries with the teaching of either language or literature in less educationally and linguistically sophisticated parts of the world; nevertheless this sum of experience provided a grounding of sympathy for and understanding of the establishment of this kind of programme at Leeds.

So much, then, for the academic and vocational sides to Contemporary English. As I have explained, the academic work stands by its own worth, while the vocational work is a collaboration with others, especially with our colleagues in Education. I come now to the sub-title to my lecture, 'A Triple Bond between Disciplines', where I hope to suggest ways in which Contemporary English interlocks with existing studies.

In the first place, and perhaps not obviously to those who are unfamiliar with recent work in British linguistics, there is here a bond between science and humanity. There are three ways in which the study of language is in contact with science: two of them are rather trivial, but one is fundamental. The trivial contacts include, first, the use of scientific equipment and therefore of scientific modes of observation and measurement in the study of language; and second, the converse of this, the use by established scientific disciplines of linguistic concepts and techniques. As examples of the first we can cite instrumental and acoustic phonetics, the use of computer techniques for grammatical and lexical analysis, research into the physiology and psychology of language, and similar work. As examples of the second we should mention communications engineering, machine translation and speech pathology.

But it is the non-trivial link I wish to stress. This lies in the nature of the linguistic theory which I have mentioned as the unifying feature of Contemporary English. I am not one who tries to equate linguistics with the physical sciences, but it remains a fact that the theory and description which inform British linguistics are in the normal line of general scientific method. Consequently our attitudes towards techniques of observation, towards our data, towards theory, description, models, measurement, experiment, are scientific at base, even though the subject of our study, language, is inherently capable of being original, creative, artistic, beautiful, miraculous. There is no antagonism between the two outlooks upon language, and I have always found my appreciation of the humane aspect of language heightened and extended by the contact I have with the scientific background of linguistic theory. This is the first bond between the disciplines.

One particular instance of the general contact I have just described constitutes my second bond, that between language and literature. As I have said, it is possible to study Contemporary English without studying the language of literature, and it is possible to study literature without studying the language used in literary works. But to carry out either task thoroughly means accepting the overlap and exploiting it. Here is an area where two disciplines interconnect, and where each can hope to contribute to the other. This is the second bond.

Finally, there is the obvious contact between the academic and the vocational spheres; between the programme of analysis and description of English on the one hand, and the programme in teaching English as a foreign language on the other. I have already explained that Contemporary English is not a department for training teachers, and that I leave this highly specialized task to my colleagues in Education. But that does not mean that I despise vocational and professional training. On the contrary, I am glad that the fruits of our academic activities can contribute to work of such crucial importance. And this is the third bond.

Bonds can pull in two directions. It is quite certain that Contemporary English, this new grouping of subjects, unified by a core of linguistic theory, will gain immeasurably in the coming years from its links with science, with literature, with education. Those of us who work in this field trust that we may be able to return, through our bonds, some repayment for the benefit we have received.